SWEDISH HERITAGE of GREATER WORCESTER

ERIC J. SALOMONSSON

THE History PRESS

Published by The History Press
Charleston, SC
www.historypress.net

First published 2015

Manufactured in the United States

ISBN 978.1.46711.942.9

Library of Congress Control Number: 2015951459

Dedicated to my family, especially my mother, Shirley, who has graciously risen to the challenge of being a "Swede by marriage."

CONTENTS

ACKNOWLEDGEMENTS

Writing a book is a journey during which one meets so many wonderful people along the way—a proverbial literary yellow brick road, if you will. Writing history allows one to become the detective. Books, newspapers and ephemera of all types, as well as archives, photographs and maps, become your best and, at times, your only friends. It's a fantastic experience, and I encourage the reader of this book to accept the challenge, be it for history or another passion.

This book is partly a revision and rewrite of a portion of an earlier MA thesis that I had written. Since that time many moons ago, more information has been uncovered, and certain inconsistencies have been corrected and updated as a result. History is never static, and neither is the researcher.

The following people helped to guide and encourage me along this journey; each provided resources and information that have helped make this story a reality. I thank you.

- The staff at the Worcester Historical Museum, especially Director William Wallace and Head Librarian Robin Christensen.
- Dr. Susan Williams (retired), Fitchburg State College.
- Professors René Reeves and Benjamin Lieberman, Fitchburg State College.
- Nancy Gaudette (retired) and the staff at the Worcester Public Library.
- Mott Lynn, head of collections management, Clark University.
- The staff of the Worcester Registry of Deeds.

- Philip Becker, Massachusetts District No. 2 Historian, Vasa Order of America.
- Millie Johnson (deceased), Trinity Lutheran Church.
- John Anderson, former mayor of Worcester.
- Members of the Worcester Swedish-American community.
- Karmen Cook, Ryan Finn and the entire staff of The History Press.
- Tom Fox, for your love and support.

INTRODUCTION

The Swedish-American historical narrative has generally become a footnote within the context of the overall American experience. With the exception of interested scholars and novice historians, that narrative is largely unknown to the academic and general public at large. Even among a great many Swedish-Americans today, there is a general lack of knowledge in terms of Swedish-American history.

It is a well-accepted fact that Vikings established a small settlement at L'Anse aux Meadows in Newfoundland in the year 1000. The Swedish presence in what would become the United States can be traced back to as early as 1638, when the colony of New Sweden was founded along the shores of the Delaware River. This founding has been the cause of celebrations for Swedes in America since 1888. The roots of the modern-day Swedish-American experience can be traced to the 1845 founding of the first permanent Swedish settlement in the Midwest, when Per Cassel and more than a dozen followers established New Sweden in Iowa. The following year, about 1,200 followers of self-proclaimed prophet Erik Jansson laid claim to Bishop Hill in Illinois, signaling an era of mass immigration. Bishop Hill is listed on the National Register of Historic Places and home to the archives of the Vasa Order of America.

During the antebellum period, the earliest arrivals settled at coastal ports or within the western interior. Eventually, large-scale Swedish immigration began, particularly in the period following the end of the American Civil

War. The lure of prime land, as promoted in the Homestead Act of 1862, attracted prospective farmers to areas in the Midwest. Despite the visions of an independent life and the romanticized visions of these immigrant settlements, the environment oftentimes proved hostile. "The elements were extreme, often violent. Most of the immigrants were ill prepared either from the burning summer sun or the icy blasts of winter in the great interior."[1] Minnesota, Illinois and Kansas, in particular, housed significant Swedish-American populations whose presence continues to influence the history and culture of the region. Groups or families, settling chiefly in the rural areas of the Midwest, characterized the earliest immigration, and many of these groups established townships that still bear their Swedish names.

TABLE 1. SWEDISH IMMIGRATION STATISTICS, 1851–1939

Decade	*Total*	*Annual Average*
1851–59	14,774	1,477
1860–69	73,570	7,357
1870–79	80,336	8,034
1880–89	331,071	33,107
1890–99	213,802	21,380
1900–1909	211,929	21,193
1910–20	98,375	9,837
1920–29	95,755	9,575
1930–39	9,133	913

Source: Figures tabulated from Lars Lindmark, *Swedish Exodus*, 145–47.

As industrialism exploded in America, the demographics of Swedish immigration changed. By the 1890s, the majority of Swedish immigrants had begun to settle within the thriving urban centers of America, particularly in the Northeast. Many were single, skilled male workers attracted by the bustling activity of the age. Single women also came in greater numbers, enticed by an independent lifestyle free from the hierarchy of Swedish everyday life. Many of these adventurous ladies became domestics and servants for those of the upper class. In time, chain migration patterns developed, fueled by kinship links. In these urban centers, of which Worcester is a prime example, the Swedes became one of a host of ethnic groups struggling to maintain cohesiveness within this new tumultuous environment. Numerous Swedish colonies were established, with large settlements in Chicago, Illinois; Jamestown, New York; and Worcester, Massachusetts. By 1910, more than half of Swedish immigrants resided in urban areas, and according to Lars Ljungmark, "this pattern has kept pace with the overall process of urbanization in American society."[2] Between 1850 and 1930, more than 1 million Swedes immigrated to the United States; about one-fifth returned to Sweden.

As the Swedish population increased, a network of national and local organizations developed in order to establish group cohesiveness within the American context. This included the foundation of social, fraternal, benevolent and religious institutions of varying denominations. Numerous weeklies and the establishment of Swedish-language publishing concerns helped to knit the local and national community together. By the turn of the twentieth century, the Swedish-American identity, in combination with the influence of American society, revealed "both the preservation of fundamental homeland values and the rejection of traditions and practices that had alienated them in Sweden."[3]

The development of an ethnic identity in America was characteristic of European-origin ethnic groups in general. Several facets of this development—including the use of national symbols, the celebration of national figures and the development of a colonial history—were key factors in the self-promotion of group identity. As the forces of industrialization and urban development increased, more and more ethnic groups found themselves in competition with one another in terms of employment, social standing and public perception. The ethnic group identity, therefore, melded national traditions into an American context. The juxtaposition of these native and American values created a uniquely distinguishable identity for the Swedes in America versus what one found in Sweden.

Although there were similarities in this Swedish-American identity construction, local and regional differences did exist. The Greater Worcester Swedish-American experience was unique in several factors; chief among them was the political relationship that developed between the Swedes and the Republican Yankee hierarchy. This relationship proved beneficial to both groups: the Republicans found a political ally in the Swedish-American community, while the Swedes were bestowed with a special status that gave them an advantage over their immigrant counterparts. Publisher and journalist Charles Nutt remarked of the Worcester Swedes, "No race has been more welcome and none has more readily adjusted itself to American standards…it is impossible to give a separate history of the Swedish people. They form a constituent part of the people of this city."[4]

Wartime and dual identity: the Swedish Folkdance Club performs at a September 1942 war bond rally in front of Worcester's city hall. *Author's collection.*

Religious considerations also weighed heavily in favor of the Swedes, as their Protestantism made them less of an anathema to the Yankee establishment. In voting, the Swedes' alignment with the Republican faction proved key when it came to issues such as the annual liquor license vote in Worcester. Swedes overall tended to be more conservative than their ethnic brethren when it came to supporting the sale of alcohol, and as such, they usually voted against the sale of liquor in the city. The development of these key identities—Republicanism, Protestantism and temperance—would define Swedish-American identity in Worcester for generations. This identity would also disrupt the ethnic chronological ethnic pecking order of "first come first served." The Irish, in particular, viewed the Swedes enviously. There had been an Irish presence in the city as early as the 1820s. Were they not entitled to certain benefits over these upstart Swedes? The Swedes, for their part, took full advantage of their favorable position, oftentimes at the expense of the Irish. It came as a shock, therefore, when their position in Worcester began to wane in the 1920s. Ethnic rivalries, at times violent, would develop, particularly between these two ethnic groups.

The Great Depression and World War II dramatically altered the fabric of the United States. The economic chaos of the 1930s affected every ethnic and racial group, while the patriotism and unity throughout the war years helped to cement a true American consensus never before experienced. The rapidly changing characteristics of American society in the postwar period transformed the Worcester Swedish-American community again, as subsequent generations found new employment outside the factory and moved out of the historical ethnic enclaves. The three key characteristics of the earlier community disappeared, to be replaced with an identity based more on symbolic practices as an American-born populace supplanted the aging immigrant community.

Despite this shift, however, the postwar period was one of increased activity for several groups. The Swedish National Federation, for example, continued to sponsor the annual Midsummer Festival and introduced an annual Lucia Ball in the early 1960s. For many organizations, the end came during the 1970s and 1980s, brought on by continued generational and societal shifts. Currently, the Swedish-American community in Worcester is characterized by a few struggling organizations and a handful of individuals who have dedicated their efforts to the preservation and maintenance of a once thriving ethnic enclave. It is also composed of individuals who are fully aware of what it means to "be Swedish," albeit they celebrate that "Swedishness" in their own personal way.

Some histories of the Worcester Swedish account end with the decline of the original characteristics of the community in the 1930s, but the community remained a viable, although transformed, entity well into the late twentieth century. However, there has been a rapid decline in the structural community within the last generation—so rapid, in fact, that most of Worcester's existing Swedish-American organizations will more than likely cease to exist within the next decade.

Hence, the structural community will be largely replaced, in many instances, with a more personal, individual identification about what it means to be "Swedish" in Worcester. Throughout many homes in the area, *Dalahästar*

Gathered together at a 1998 Swedish festival. *From left to right*: Thurston Solomon, Krystle Briggs, Kris Briggs, Dawn Briggs, Gladys Landquist and Shirley Solomon. *Author's collection.*

(Dala horses) and a Swedish flag decorate the corner shelf, while at Christmas, *glögg* or *sill* is consumed while wishing friends and family members *God Jul* (Merry Christmas). Some may attend a festival. Vehicles may even sport a Swedish decal of some sort. These "bumper sticker Swedes," as Finnish-American historian Barry Heiniluoma called them, feel this small homage to their ancestry to be enough. With others, a trip to Sweden or genealogical research helps to bring them closer with living relatives and ancestors long passed, while others may be actively engaged in the preservation of history and heritage. This book is an example of that. The more individual identification is reflected in varying degrees. Such is the changing face of community; such is the changing face of Swedish Worcester.

Chapter 1

GREATER WORCESTER AND THE SWEDES

Worcester

In the Worcester context, an unparalleled era of industrial growth forms the groundwork of immigration to the city. The arrival of the first documented Swede, Carl (Charles) Hanson in 1868, coincided with the rapid industrial growth of the city. This in itself does not make the Swedish experience unique, for by this time burgeoning industrial growth had already made Worcester a magnet for various immigrant groups, such as the Irish and French-Canadians. However, it was the Swedes who quickly rose to prominence in this era. "If one ethnic group were to be singled out, one group whose history coincided with the grandest era of the city, it would be the Swedish."[5]

Worcester, by 1900, seemed to have it all—a prime geographic location and an extremely successful diversified industrial base. The arrival of the railroad into this predominantly agricultural town in 1835 signaled that changes were on the horizon. Within thirty years, industrialization and the resulting urbanization had transformed the cultural landscape of the once agricultural town. Worcester was incorporated as a city in 1848. Throughout the following decade, "the city reported growing concentrations in textiles, wire production, machine shops, and boot and shoe manufacturing."[6] The railroad maintained shipping costs at a minimum, and combined with a prime geographic location, the city rapidly developed into a regional trading and industrial center. Population growth followed suit. In 1850, the newly incorporated town housed 17,000 residents; twenty years later, more than 40,000 lived in the growing industrial city. The period between 1890 and 1900 saw a population explosion; over that ten-year period, the population jumped from 84,655 to 118,421. The city continued its explosive growth, and by 1920, the population stood at 179,754.

Very quickly, this commercial hub became one of the most heterogeneous industrial centers in the country. Immigrants constituted more than 20 percent of the city's population by 1865. An 1893 overview of the city's school system reported, "We have all varieties of Scandinavians, as in Quinsigamond. Finns and Russian Jews crowd other localities, while Armenians, Turks, Arabs, Africans…and even Chinese children, may be found in certain schools…What was once an almost homogenous people has become nearly as polyglot as that which fills the school rooms of some parts of New York."[7]

By the dawn of the twentieth century, Worcester had morphed into an industrial powerhouse, producing the greatest amount of manufactured goods in the country. City companies turned out adjustable wrenches and an array of machine tools; lawn mowers, grinding wheels and abrasive products; and wire and wire-related products. There were pool tables, underwear and corsets, pistols and shotguns, wrought-iron products, roller skates, bricks, valentine cards, beer and stained glass. By the 1890s, the country's largest carpet and skate manufacturers were located in Worcester, as were the leading producers of industrial looms and envelopes. In addition, the city housed the largest wire factory in the world.

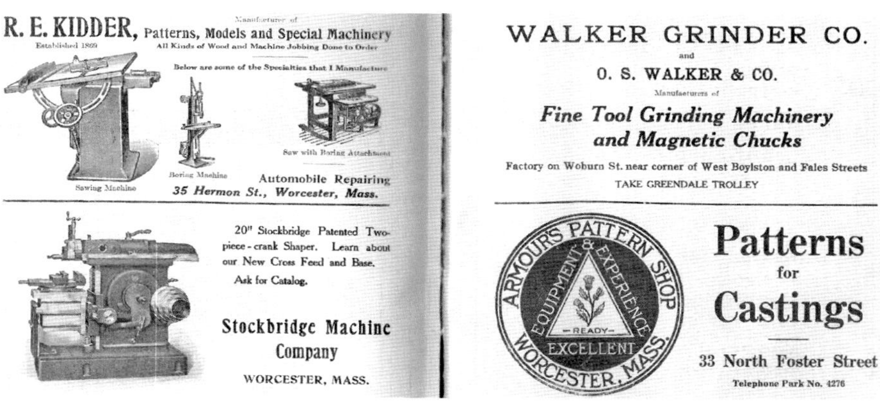

Readers of the 1915 Worcester City Directory could find myriad industrial products for sale, indicative of Worcester's manufacturing diversity. *Author's collection.*

In 1898, Worcester celebrated the fiftieth anniversary of its incorporation as a city—from a largely agrarian town of about 15,000 to an industrial city teeming with more than 115,000 in fifty years. The growth, to many residents, seemed remarkable. "Few municipalities have within any single half century been more favored in everything which could contribute to material prosperity, local expansion, and real advancement in the line of human progress. In the growth of the city, the most sanguine expectations have been exceeded and the most extravagant predictions fulfilled."[8] The tower of the newly opened city hall, soaring more than two hundred feet above Main Street's business district, epitomized Worcester's progress. It

Worcester's impressive city hall as it appeared circa 1900. By this time, Worcester was in the midst of rapid economic and social change. *Author's collection.*

had been a remarkable journey indeed, and Worcester residents looked confidently toward the future.

In that semi-centennial year, the city housed more than 1,400 industrial establishments employing more than 21,700 people. Industrial expansion continued well into the twentieth century. By 1914, estimates placed the number of Worcester manufacturing concerns at approximately 2,500, employing more than 30,000. In the city, a unique system of small- and medium-sized shops developed, most of which employed no more than 50 persons. According to one source, by 1895, "the average number of employees in Worcester's 1,415 firms was 15."[9] Only two sprawling manufacturing complexes existed: Norton Company in Greendale and American Steel and Wire, with plants on Grove Street (Northworks) and in Quinsigamond Village (Southworks).[10] It was around these two giant companies that many of the Worcester Swedes settled.

The city's cultural landscape included dozens of churches representing numerous ethnic and religious denominations. French-Canadians, Polish, Irish and Italians organized their separate Catholic parishes, while the black community worshipped under the banner of the African Methodist Episcopal Church. The first Armenian church in the United States, the Church of Our Savior, was established in Worcester in 1891. The Jews established several synagogues and societies, while Seventh Day Adventist, Episcopal and Presbyterian congregations served hundreds of others. The Swedes and their churches shall be the topic of a later discussion.

New schools were erected rapidly to keep pace with the burgeoning student population. More than two dozen were constructed during the 1890s, while numerous existing schoolhouses were enlarged. In 1898 alone, the city council appropriated $160,000 for schoolhouse construction—a large sum for the times when one considers that the average elementary schoolhouse cost approximately $30,000 to erect. By 1901, the most modern and largest of the county's high schools, South High on Richards Street, had been completed and occupied. To ready the vocational workers of the future, the city, at the behest of industrial leaders, opened Boys' Trade (1910) and Girls' Trade (1911) high schools. Across the city, institutes of higher learning included Clark University, Worcester Polytechnic Institute and Holy Cross College.

It is a great credit to Worcester that no true slums or ethnic ghettos developed. Instead, three-deckers were constructed beginning in the 1860s to cope with the burgeoning population. This type of dwelling proved so popular that by the 1890s, three-deckers accounted for more than half

In order to prepare a skilled workforce for the future, industrial leaders encouraged the city to organize the Boys' Trade School, which opened in 1910. *Author's collection.*

of all new homes constructed. Originally erected within walking distance of manufactories, three-deckers soon spread across the city, as the public transportation network made it possible to live farther from the workplace. By the time the last three-decker was constructed in 1932, about six thousand had been built in Worcester. According to Marilyn Spear, the three-decker had formed "like calcium deposits along the 'spines' which radiated from the city's industrial plants." Such dwellings successfully "met the needs of workingmen and their families."[11]

Practically every neighborhood had at least one park, with most encompassing a scenic body of water and other amenities. Green Hill was the gem of the park system, encompassing more than five hundred acres. Donald Tulloch, echoing the spirit of civic pride, remarked in the introduction to his book *Worcester: City of Prosperity* that he, as with others, had "been taken recently to eulogize Worcester in all its attractiveness, and place it in the estimate of the world where it rightly belongs—as one of the most kingly cities to be born in, to be educated in, to toil in, to die in and to be buried in (for even Worcester's cemeteries are very attractive looking), and to go to heaven from."[12]

It was in this growing industrial city that Carl Hanson, generally considered the first recorded Swede, settled with his family in Worcester.

Three-deckers were constructed in response to Worcester's population boom; the examples seen here are in the Belmont Hill neighborhood. *Author's collection.*

Hanson, born in Uddevalla in the province of Bohuslän, had settled initially in Boston following his arrival in America. He married in that capital city, and in the fall of 1868, he and his family arrived in Worcester. Due to this distinction and to his establishment of a successful music store, Hanson became a symbol of the Worcester Swedish-American success story. He was, however, far from being its leading spokesman; on the contrary, Hanson became a master at the art of dual identity. He ingeniously learned to balance Swedish and American roles, playing each part as conditions warranted. In advertising, for example, Hanson was known as "Carl" in Swedish-American publications, while similarly assuming the Anglicized "Charles" in the American press. In her study of Hanson, Anne-Charlotte Harvey noted, "What we find suggests a simultaneous cultivation of an ethnic and assimilated profile. Hanson could be either, or both, when it suited him…one wonders whether the label 'first Swede in Worcester' may have been an obligation, a role he had to play, or a business advantage he could not do without."[13] With this perplexing dual identity, it's not surprising that Hanson, a skilled musician and author, chose to be buried at Hope Cemetery rather than at the neighboring Swedish Cemetery across the street.

A small group of Swedish potters and their families arrived soon after Hanson, settling originally in the neighborhood around Water Street and finding employment at Frank B. Norton's pottery shop on the aforementioned street. Included among this group was Maria Frodigh, the first Swedish woman to settle in Worcester. In 1875, another band of Swedes, Methodists from the Michigan iron district of Ishpeming, settled in the Quinsigamond Village neighborhood, within the shadow of the Washburn and Moen Southworks plant.

Carl (Charles) Hanson is regarded as the first recorded Swede in Worcester. Hanson assumes a striking pose in this circa 1885 portrait. *Author's collection.*

The First Swedish Methodist Church in Quinsigamond Village, as pictured in 1928. The historic church was rebuilt following a disastrous fire in 1977. *Author's collection.*

Experienced industrial workers, these Methodist Swedes received a "warm welcome…from Yankees in the Village," and this led them to promote the immigration of fellow Swedes from both Michigan and their home parish in Karlskoga, Sweden.[11] These Methodists established the First Swedish Methodist Church in Worcester, the first church of its kind in both the city and New England. They also proved themselves of the outmost importance in the success of their denomination in the region. One account, in fact, stated that Worcester was "the city which has proved to be the most fruitful field for Swedish Methodism."[15]

Despite the arrival of these groups of immigrants, the Swedish population did not grow rapidly in that first decade. By 1876, the entire "Scandinavian" population stood at about 166. This number likely included Norwegians and Danes as well. However, four years later, in 1880, it had swelled to around 1,000. Apparently there was enough of a population to warrant the publication of a directory. The 1883 *Kalender Öfver Svenskarne i Worcester* (*Almanac of the Swedish in Worcester*) listed the Swedish residents, by then having doubled, but the editors apologized that this register was not entirely accurate (translation by author):

> *Vi hade önskat få kalendern fullständig, men i anseende till den korta tid vi haft, och en del personers vägran att lemna sina namn, hafva vi icke kunnat få den så fullständig som vi velat. Den upptager dock omkring 2000 namn, deraf ett betydligt angtal å i Quinsigamond bosatte svenskar.*
>
> [We had wished to have the almanac complete, but in considering the short time we had, and on the part of persons who refused to give their name, we have not been able to complete it as we had wanted. There are around 2000 names included, among those a considerable number of Swedes who have settled at Quinsigamond.][16]

The growth of Quinsigamond Village, the earliest Swedish enclave, is a prime example of ethnic neighborhood development as articulated by ethnic historian Kathleen Neils Conzen. She has stated that in ethnic neighborhoods, "a simple desire to live among persons speaking the same language and sharing a similar culture" was not the only factor influencing its development. More often than not, additional causes included "migration chains and common occupations and incomes dictating similar residential locations."[17] The development of the main Swedish enclaves in Worcester followed along these lines. As in the case of the Village, the Swedish communities that developed in the upper Vernon Hill, upper Belmont Hill and Greendale neighborhoods centered primarily on large industrial centers that were the major source of employment for the Swedish immigrants, many of them skilled in the trades. In addition, the Quinsigamond Swedes were largely residents of the province of Värmland, while natives of the southern Swedish province of Skåne, particularly from the town of Höganäs, predominated in Greendale.

By 1890, there were 4,558 recorded Swedish-born in the city; the population had become large enough by this time to warrant the establishment of a mercantile co-op store, local publications, six congregations and the Swedish Cemetery Corporation. Ten years later, the number of Swedish-born reached 7,992.

The Swedish-born population of Worcester peaked in the 1915 Massachusetts census at slightly over 8,100 and falling to 7,751 by 1920 and 7,579 by 1930. The declining numbers were a result of several factors, most notably the advent of the First World War, which drastically curtailed overall immigration to the United States; immigration quotas established by the United States in the 1920s; and the passing of the older members of the community. Improving conditions within Sweden as it entered into the age of the Social Democrats and the Welfare State also contributed to this decline. By 1940, the number of Swedish-born stood at 6,641, and by 1970, native Swedish residents numbered no fewer than 2,000.

As indicated in the following table, Worcester quickly became a Swedish mecca in Massachusetts, housing on average 80 percent of the Swedish-born in Worcester County and more than 20 percent of the state's Swedish-born residents.

TABLE 2. SWEDISH-BORN

	1870	*1880*	*1890*	*1900*	*1910*	*1920*	*1930*	*1940*
Worcester	19	848	4,558	7,992	8,036	7,751	7,579	6,641
Worcester County	62	1,060	5,633	9,825	10,580	10,215	10,210	7,649
Massachusetts	1,386	4,756	18,624	32,192	39,560	38,012	36,810	28,128

Source: Unites States Census records.

The first official decennial (every ten years) census in Massachusetts took place in 1855, and for the researcher, the statistics available have proven to be a wealth of information. The statistics compiled are exhaustive in nature, but historically, they reflect a state in the midst of rapid demographic and social change. The following table, compiled through available statistics, gives the reader an idea of the dramatic growth of the Swedish community through first- and second-generation figures. These figures seem to line up with popular accounts, which estimate that by 1920 one in five Worcester residents was of Swedish lineage.

TABLE 3. WORCESTER

	1895	*1905*	*1915*
Native-born with one or both parents Swedish-born	2,567	13,411	20,936
Swedish-born	6,624	7,992	8,150
First and second generation total	9,280	21,403	29,086
Worcester Population	98,767	128,135	162,697
Percent Swedish	9.3%	16.7%	17.8%

Source: Decennial Census of Massachusetts records.

As early as 1910, John P. Holmgren estimated that the "Scandinavian people" in Worcester numbered "fully 30,000."[18] Indeed, sixteen years later, the *Worcester Evening Post* stated that Worcester had "at the present time more than 30,000 Swedish-speaking people."[19] Prominent local historian Charles Nutt estimated the "Scandinavian" population in 1910 at about twenty-five thousand and about thirty thousand eight years later. Later accounts run higher. For example, a 1953 article noted, "Interestingly, in this city and its suburbs numbering some 276,000 persons, approximately 45,000 of them are of Swedish descent."[20] The author does not document the source for this figure, leaving the researcher to ponder whether this is but a hypothesis on the author's part. In 1958, professor Robert Beck of Clark University estimated that in 1920, Worcester had twenty thousand native-born and the same number of second-generation Swedes.

The latter two estimates leave much to consider. In trying to compile accurate numbers, different variables must be taken into account. For example, if the term "Scandinavian" is used, did the number include the smaller populations of Norwegians and Danes or even Finns? The term "Swedish-speaking" is rather ambiguous and perhaps took into account the Swede-Finn community as well. In addition, third and subsequent generations may have also been included, although the time frame of the earlier estimates limits this possibility, and recorded statistics of the third generation do not exist.

One 1930 article that appeared in *Svea* apparently questioned popular assessments, citing that the Worcester area's Swedish-Americans were "estimated at 25,000 to 40,000 people." This last figure was called into question as "no doubt too high." The writer did believe, however, that "safely stated," a true estimate did "not fall below 30,000."[21]

Of the towns surrounding Worcester, Auburn and Holden housed the largest Swedish-American communities. Smaller settlements existed in Shrewsbury and Millbury, but in the case of the latter, this was due largely to the presence of a significant summer colony that sprang up around the shores of Ramshorn Pond. Particularly for Auburn and Holden, active Swedish-American communities had developed by the 1920s.

With the exception of Auburn, most of the towns originally housed small mills, which were scattered in various locations. In Holden, for example, mills were found in the Jefferson, Quinapoxet and Dawson sections. Most of the early immigrant labor consisted of Irish and French-Canadian immigrants who had arrived to fill the low-paying vacancies in these mills. There was a tendency for the native-born of suburban towns to seek better employment in Worcester. As a result, the demographics of the surrounding towns began to change, and foreign-born workers began to constitute greater percentages of the population.[22]

The continued urbanization of Worcester also affected these suburban areas. The city environs had so expanded southward that by 1900, it had already affected neighboring Auburn. The northwestern portion of that town became a satellite of Worcester and developed more rapidly than other areas. The same settlement pattern affected other townships as well.

The progression of technology resulted in the growth and expansion of train, streetcar and, eventually, bus service to the surrounding towns. By the 1920s, development of the automobile had dramatically altered the perception of distance and time. Coinciding with the popularity of the automobile was the continued expansion of the infrastructure. Existing roads were improved, and new roads were developed. The state highway connecting Worcester and Holden, for example, was completed in 1928. One researcher noted that with these transformations, it became difficult to distinguish the city with bordering suburban districts. Moreover, the expansion continued and accelerated following the end of World War II, as new housing developments, such as Winthrop Oaks in Holden, were constructed. The post–World War II period saw a major exodus to the suburbs. As a result, second-generation churches were established. Thus, Christ Lutheran Church in West Boylston and Mount Olivet Church in Shrewsbury had, as charter members, many Swedish-Americans, as well as new converts to the Lutheran faith. Unlike their predecessors, these congregations were truly "American" in composition.

Originally, farming constituted a part-time occupation for many town residents. Throughout the period of suburban development, Worcester remained the primary source of employment for the Swedish-American population. The proximity of the Norton Company to Holden, for example, played a role in the settlement pattern of the Swedish-Americans within this town. Swedish immigrants could be found in the four aforementioned towns as early as 1885. A brief overview of Swedish settlement in these areas shall now be discussed.

Holden

According to the state census for 1885, Holden housed 64 Swedish-born residents, the largest settlement of the surrounding towns. By 1905, the Swedish-born population had increased to 154, while the second generation swelled the ethnic community to more than double that number. A decade later, first- and second-generation Swedes numbered 654. As early as the turn of the twentieth century, a small chapel had been constructed at Chaffins, the town's primary Swedish district and named the Scandinavian Evangelical Congregational Church. Population figures cannot be found for 1925, although one researcher estimated the entire community at slightly fewer than 1,200 persons, this increase resulting from the growth of the second generation rather than new immigration. The Immanuel Lutheran Church was constructed in the 1920s on land donated by the C.J. Hultgren family to serve the growing Lutheran population. Others attended the neighboring Congregational church.

By the post–World War II period, a second phase had begun as many Worcester Swedes relocated to Holden. As one researcher remarked in 1951, "Several times…the statement was made by Swedish people that, 'the Swedes are moving to Holden.' It seems that many people of this group desire to live in sparsely settled sections, probably more so than peoples of most other cultural groups."[23] The proximity of the Norton Company to Holden may also explain this movement, as many city workers strived to own homes in the suburbs. Although Swedish-Americans settled into areas throughout the town, for several decades the Chaffins section of Holden remained the primary Swedish-American enclave.

AUBURN

There were but 13 Swedish-born residents living in Auburn according to the 1885 census; in 1905, first- and second-generation Swedes numbered 348. By 1915, the Swedish community numbered over 850 and composed a quarter of the town's population. A 1937 centennial history noted that Auburn was "like many New England towns" in ethnic makeup. However, "next to the Yankee group, which is the largest in town, come the Swedish-Americans who number about eight hundred."[24] The Swedish-Americans of Auburn developed into a comprehensive ethnic community, particularly in the northwestern section of town, as in Stoneville.

By 1925, both the Bethel Lutheran congregation and a social organization known as *Skogsblomman* (Forest Flower) had been founded. This group constructed a summer clubhouse and dance hall on Bylund Avenue along the shore of Rotary Pond about 1922. In 1926, the Scandinavian Peoples' Park Association, a subsidiary of the Scandinavian Workers' Trade Union, constructed a summer dance hall and clubhouse in Auburn at Trowbridgeville Lake (now Leesville Pond). Monies used in the construction of the "Peoples' Park" project were raised "through loans and donations from members and sympathizers."[25] Socialist in nature,

The new Bethel Lutheran Church shortly after its 1960 opening. This replaced the original wooden church at the same site. *Author's collection.*

this Worcester-based organization was founded in 1893, though little information remains on it. This park was located within the Trowbridgeville district on the Auburn-Worcester line, itself a Swedish-American enclave. In 1928, a local lodge of the Vasa Order of America was organized: Charles Lindbergh No. 520, in honor of the famous aviator.

Two of the more notable businesses in town were the Oscar Sjogren and Son Tool and Machine Company on Sword Street at Trowbridgeville and Holstrom's Market, which operated in the center of town at Drury Square, for years the town's major intersection. Holstrom's was one of the earlier markets to offer delivery services. Family members have restored the market's delivery truck, an area staple fondly remembered by residents. It is occasionally entered in area vintage car shows.

Most of the icons of Swedish-Auburn had disappeared by the 1980s. Charles Lindbergh No. 520 relocated in the early 1960s to Worcester, where it disbanded years later. Skogsblomman Inc. closed in the early 1980s, and its clubhouse was converted to a private residence. The Peoples' Park had long been demolished by this time. Bethel Lutheran remains a vibrant and active, albeit mainstream, congregation.

Millbury and Shrewsbury

Although both of these towns housed Swedish populations, they were smaller than the communities of Auburn or Holden. The 1885 census recorded 41 Swedish-born persons in Millbury, while Shrewsbury housed only 4; by 1915, first- and second-generation Swedes numbered 662 and 296, respectively. The increase in Shrewsbury was noted by Balk, who stated that "Swedes and Italians were becoming more prominent in the census figures" by 1915.[26]

The scenic beauty around Lake Quinsigamond prompted several Worcester-based organizations to purchase property and erect clubhouses in Shrewsbury. The earliest of these was the summer headquarters of the Svea Gille social club. This multistoried, turreted building, described by one source as "the largest and most beautiful club house among the Swedes in the United States," was dedicated in 1894 at Lake Quinsigamond and for years was popular with both Swedes and non-Swedes.[27] The clubhouse was torn down and replaced with condominiums in the 1980s.

For generations, the impressive Svea Gille clubhouse at Lake Quinsigamond was a popular meeting place for area Swedish-Americans. *Author's collection.*

In 1928, the Scandinavian Athletic Club purchased land and through fundraising efforts was able to construct athletic fields and a unique domed clubhouse on Lake Street the following year. The club hoped "to make the field a community center for all Scandinavian recreational and athletic events, as well as for any other purposes…where out-of-town visitors may also be welcomed."[28] For years, the annual Swedish Midsummer Festival has been held on its grounds. Today, the facility, commonly referred to as "SAC Park," continues to abide by its original purpose, albeit a less ethnic one, and remains a popular facility for hosting public and private events.

A small Swedish community developed in the Edgemere section of Shrewsbury along Lake Quinsigamond. During the 1920s, the Scandinavian Women's Gymnastics Club operated a clubhouse here. In 1923, the Edgemere Lodge, under the proprietorship of Ellen A. Russell and Anna C. Anderson, opened; it became a destination for local Swedish-Americans. *Svea* reported in an issue on July 11 that the lodge was located in one of the finest and most scenic areas of the lake and noted that the "*nyöppnade svenska pensionatet, som en kär till flyktsort for varandren*" ("newly opened Swedish boardinghouse, is a cherished escape for the traveler"). In addition, *Svea* noted (translation by author):

> *Edgemere lodge fyller ett särskildt för oss svenskar länge känt behof af en svensk restaurant af allra förstklassigaste slag, hvilket man hade nöjet konstatera efter en middag å platsen förliden söndag.*
>
> [Edgemere Lodge fills a special need for us Swedes long in need of a Swedish restaurant of the best in first class description, which one must call attention to after a pleasant lunch at that locality last Sunday afternoon.]

In Millbury, the greatest concentration of Swedes could be found along Ramshorn Pond in the north of town not far from the Worcester line. This settlement was originally seasonal, as numerous Swedes from neighboring Quinsigamond Village in Worcester constructed summer cottages along its shore. In time, many of these cottages were transformed into year-round quarters, several of which are occupied by descendants of the original families.

One of the larger employers in Millbury at one time was the New England High Carbon Wire Company, founded by Carl Thure Lund in 1923. Lund himself lived in Quinsigamond Village. The company employed 325 workers by the late 1950s and was one of the largest importers of Swedish steel rods at the time.

There were no religious edifices constructed in either town by the Swedish-American population. In Shrewsbury, the Mount Olivet Lutheran congregation was organized in 1954. Although established as a mainstream congregation in the postwar period, Swedish-Americans figured prominently in the makeup of the congregation at the time of its inception, and an annual Lucia Fest was held for several years after the establishment of the church. The following chart highlights 1915 statistics for the aforementioned towns.

TABLE 4. 1915 FIGURES

	Auburn	*Holden*	*Millbury*	*Shrewsbury*
First- and second-generation figures	857	654	662	296
Town population	3,281	2,514	5,265	2,794
Percent Swedish	26.1%	26%	12.5%	10.5%

Source: Figures tabulated from Decennial Census of Massachusetts.

Chapter 2

IDENTITY AND THE ETHNIC TRANSFORMATION

The Swedish-American ethnic identity has been transformed by several factors, including the generational, demographic and societal makeup of American society. In fact, the "Indian summer" of Swedish-America was over by 1940, according to historian Arnold Barton. Almost twenty years later, in 1959, the Worcester newspaper *Svea* proclaimed that Swedish-America as an entity was "no more than a shadow" of its former self and predicted an early demise without a concentrated effort to sustain it.[29] Despite this outlook, there were earlier pundits who prophesized that not only Swedish-America but also the Swedish language would survive the twentieth century. Noted Gustav Andreen in 1900 (translation by author):

> *Våra fader trodde först, att svenskan skulle vara död inom en tjugo, sedan trettio, säkert inom femtio år. Nu har femtio år förflutit, och under denna tid har det blott gått framåt, sa att svenskan talas och läses nu Amerika af flere än någonsin förr.*
>
> [Our fathers thought first that Swedish should be dead within twenty, then thirty, surely within fifty years. Now fifty years have passed and during this time it has gone forward, so that Swedish is spoken and read now in America more than anytime before.]

Andreen then noted that the Swedes had "already built up the monuments" of a presence in America and encouraged the succeeding generations to "forever be a testimony to *sitt nordiska ursprung* [your Nordic origin]."[30] Andreen, however, wrote these words at a time when Swedish immigration to America was at a peak.

Ten years later, clergyman Baptist clergyman Karl Karlson noted how the language transition was affecting the community in Worcester. He observed that Swedes who arrived in America after the age of thirty never fully developed a fluency in the English language. "He may learn to understand it and speak it passably," he stated, "but he will in most cases prefer to speak his mother tongue when the other party can understand him."

Karlson felt that this was the case with many families in which the parents were Swedish-born and the children raised in America. Swedish may be the language at home, but eventually English dominated outside the home. "From this time on there is a strife in the child's mind about which language he is going to use and most naturally he settles this strife in favor of the English." The pressures facing these American-born children were numerous, Karlson felt, and included peer pressure at school and fear of speaking a foreign language outside the home.

This subsequent loss of Swedish, Karlson went on, affected the relationship between parents and children. "Swedish is dropped more and more, and in the same degree it is dropped there rises a bar between the older and younger generation because the older people do not speak English well enough to pass criticism." He lamented the decline in Swedish, especially since the beauty of Swedish literature was a victim of this transition and indicated "half of the world is missing for the Swedish-American youth. If he understood what he looses when he drops the Swedish language he surely would not do it."[31] The Swedish language was one of the unifying facets of the early ethnic community in Worcester. As the language waned, the idea of being "Swedish" in Worcester underwent transformations as well.

Indeed, the language question was the focus of debate within Swedish-American circles throughout the country during the first quarter of the twentieth century and reached its zenith during the 1930s, when the last debates occurred within the national Swedish-American hierarchy, most notably between Dr. Johannes Hoving and Vilhelm Berger. Hoving was a rather peculiar individual. He believed in the strength and purity of race as a basis for ethnic maintenance and promoted the study of eugenics. To Hoving, preservation of both the racial stock and the mother tongue was the only way in which to uphold the Swedish heritage in America. In one 1933 article, Hoving publicly attacked Vilhelm Berger, editor of the Swedish-American newspaper *Nordstjernan* in New York. He disputed Berger's claims

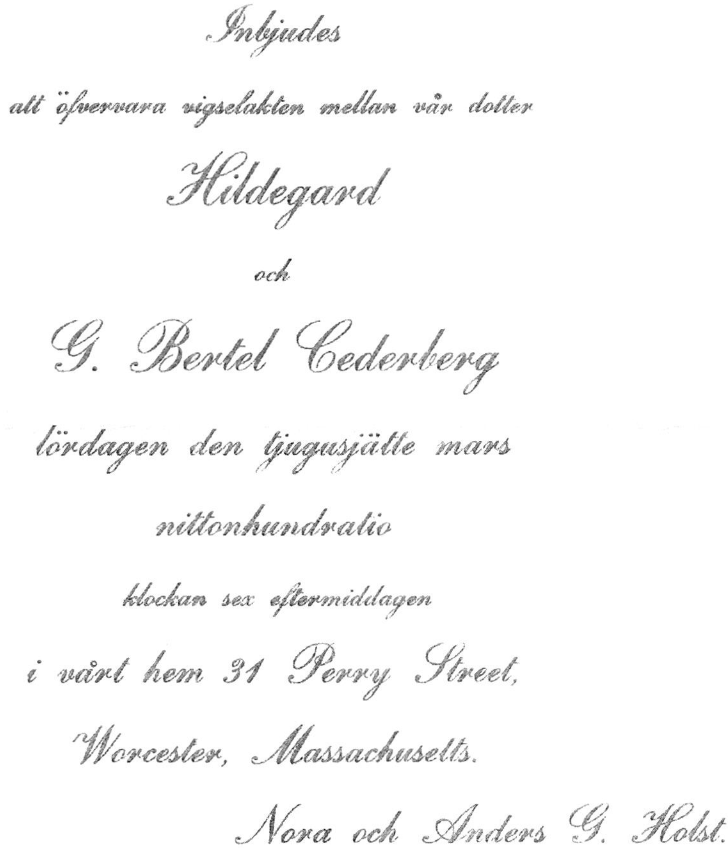

Inbjudes

att öfvervara vigselakten mellan vår dotter

Hildegard

och

G. Bertel Cederberg

lördagen den tjugusjätte mars

nittonhundratio

klockan sex eftermiddagen

i vårt hem 31 Perry Street,

Worcester, Massachusetts.

Nora och Anders G. Holst.

The 1910 wedding invitation of Hildegard Holst and G. Bertel Cederberg illustrated the importance of language within the early ethnic community. *Author's collection.*

that the Swedish language was not necessary in the long-term maintenance of a Swedish-American identity. Berger himself dismissed Hoving and other pundits who believed that "the Swedish heritage and the Swedish language are like a pair of Siamese twins who must remain joined in order to live." Berger was content to let the language issue solve itself. "That of which the heart is full," he remarked, "the mouth will speak. Let each one speak the language in which he or she is best able to express his or her thoughts."[32] Berger believed that instead of focusing unnecessary energies on the language issue, Swedish-Americans should concentrate on the preservation of both the historical and cultural aspects of the community.

By 1940, many secular and religious organizations had bowed to the inevitable and incorporated English into their activities on a piecemeal basis. This movement gained momentum throughout and following the Second World War and reflected societal transformations within the Swedish-American community. This transformation was not unique to the ethnic community but instead reflected an American society in flux.

The heyday of Swedish-America occurred during the first two decades of the twentieth century. Thereafter social, cultural and political changes within the United States transformed the community. The pressures of World War I, xenophobia, immigration restriction and the aging of the immigrant generation placed undue pressures on the community by the 1920s. The Swedish-American experience was not unique; other European-origin ethnic groups at the time experienced the same pressures. Indeed, the forces that existed within the country at the time of World War I decimated the German-American community, an immigrant group that had, according to professor Kathleen Neils Conzen, developed a successful formula of remaining ethnically German and politically American.

Fortunately, the Worcester Swedish-American community was spared the injustices of the forced Americanization campaigns that arose from the tensions of World War I, largely because of its unique relationship with the local Yankee hierarchy. In many instances, the ethnic community flourished. The Swedes of Worcester, however, did not escape the ensuing tensions of the 1920s, a decade of rapid social transformation in American society. In an attempt to preserve their special place in Worcester, many Swedes, like many Americans, gravitated toward the Ku Klux Klan as a political move. Although this was but a brief flirtation, this action affected ethnic relations for the remainder of the decade. Thus the violence that characterized the Klan's appearance in Worcester was a prelude to even greater confrontations between the Swedish and, in particular, the Irish.

The Swedish-American community in Worcester seems to have passed through three distinct phases:

1. Settlement through 1900. The establishment of early social, musical and religious organizations occurred. Many of these fledgling groups survived no more than a few years. Many were Scandinavian and not wholly Swedish, as the numbers of each ethnic group were not sufficient enough to warrant separate organizations. Early Swedish-language publications were also established and disbanded. By the

The founding of the Swedish Lutheran Old People's Home in 1920 represented both Swedish-American compassion and the aging of the immigrant generation. *Author's collection.*

1890s, the development of a tripartite ethnic identity had taken root: Republican, Protestant and temperate.

2. The maturing of the community occurred during the 1920s, exemplified by the expansion of established social, religious and benevolent institutions. The network stretched outside city limits as established suburban communities expanded their networks. These suburban networks were often tied to the Worcester community. The establishment of the Swedish Lutheran Old People's Home signified the aging of the immigrant generation. The social, political and ethnic characteristics of the city were transformed during the decade, directly affecting Swedish-American identity.
3. By the 1980s, the community experienced a dramatic decline as organizations folded, merged or continued at a much-reduced level of activity. Surviving associations today face an uncertain future. However, a sense of "Swedishness" cannot be measured accurately, given the fluctuating and personal nature of ethnicity today.

As mentioned previously, structurally the community entered into a period of sustained growth during the 1920s. Despite the activity, there were signs of impending changes from within: church services were increasingly using

Crowds may be smaller, but Midsummer is still celebrated throughout the Worcester area, as seen here in this 2002 photo taken at Sovittaja Park in Rutland. *Author's collection.*

"the American language," immigration had slowed to a trickle due to improving conditions in Sweden and the passage of immigration quotas and the New England Lutheran Synod had established the Swedish Lutheran Old People's Home on Harvard Street in the city in response to the aging immigrant generation. These changes together would, in effect, alter the demographic makeup of the community. Despite this, Swedish-Americans remained an integral part of the cultural landscape in the Worcester area.

In researching the transformation of the Worcester Swedish-American community, one contradictory factor should be noted. The community is not a separate entity any longer, and yet vestiges remain to state that a total assimilation—or, more accurately, absorption—is incomplete at this time. Ethnic geographer Werner Sollors best described this phenomenon in 1981 as "the incorporation of un-American Americanness." This phenomenon is highlighted throughout the Worcester area with small celebrations marking specific Swedish traditions, such as Midsummer (the longest day of the year), Lucia (the shortest day of the year) or Julotta (early morning Christmas service). As of 2014, Nordic Lodge No. 611 of the Vasa Order and the Finnish Heritage Society Sovittaja (Rutland, Massachusetts) still sponsor well-attended Scandinavian dinner dances throughout the year. Yet these all these festivities occur within a truly American context.

Despite the outward appearance of an active community, just what will the next generation bring? This question is by no means representative of the Worcester Swedish-American experience; ethnic communities across the country face an uncertain future. This "ethnic crisis," as defined by Stephen Steinberg, is related to numerous factors: "Specifically, the three institutions that served as the pillars of traditional society, and of the ethnic community in particular—the family, the church, and the local community—have all been weakened in terms of their authority over the lives of individuals."[33] Facing such overwhelming odds, can ethnic communities survive overall? In short, although there are some outward signs in the Worcester area to suggest that the Swedish-American ethnic identity is still a viable one, the time is approaching when public manifestations of an ethnic heritage will disappear. When this occurs, the structural community will have at last reached the point of complete absorption into American society.

But there is another dimension to the role of ethnic identity. Critics will argue that the European-origin ethnic identities continue to survive, despite the pressures of modern American society. Many will point to studies and interviews that suggest strong ethnic feelings shared by many Americans and that such feelings belie the assimilation model. Terms such as H. Arnold Barton's "elective ethnicity" and Marilyn Halter's "portable ethnicity" are used to support the theory that ethnic identity today remains a strong rallying point for many Americans. What such research has proven is that ethnic identity today is fluid—it has become an aspect of individual taste that can be celebrated or discarded at will. Such ethnic identification, however, is not strong enough to maintain the structural ethnic community. The maintenance of such a community must go beyond *feeling* ethnic; there must be an *effort* involved in *sustaining* a particular ethnic identity. Thus, as the last structural components of the local Swedish-American community struggle to survive, the trend continues toward a more personal vision of what it means to be Swedish-American in Worcester. In this new Internet age, will social media fill a void for those longing to "be Swedish"? In January 2015, the "Swedes from Worcester County, Massachusetts" page was organized on Facebook. Recipes, personal anecdotes, historical information and familial links are topics of discussion. In a sense, this microcosm on Facebook has begun the process of bringing fellow "Swedes" together, albeit digitally, to share in the common bonds of ethnic identity. Will sites such as this be the twenty-first-century version of the church supper or dinner dance of old?

Vasa members Eleanor Vincelette, Marge Stake, Gladys and William Landquist, Eric J. Salomonsson, Gulla Magnusson, Dawn Briggs and Norma Belden bedecked in folk costumes, 2002. Will social media replace gatherings such as these? *Author's collection.*

This is food for thought. The idea of community has been transformed over time. Perhaps the community of the future may require no organizational structure or hierarchy; rather, it will be purely symbolic and based on representations, ideals and traditions that were themselves the product of earlier ethnic group self-promotional campaigns. This developing concept, as Mary C. Waters stated, "meets a need Americans have for community without individual cost."[34] Therefore, the new ethnic community may be as fluid as the modern ethnic identity; they will have both entered into the realm of the abstract.

Chapter 3

BEING SWEDISH IN WORCESTER

Creation and Crisis

Various components went into the construction and promotion of a Swedish-American identity. It must be remembered that the Swedes entered a Worcester that was teeming with social, ethnic and political divisions that made the atmosphere in Worcester "intricate and variegated."[35] Coerced by the existing framework, the immigrant Swedes had no choice but to develop a unique identity based on these divisions. The initial identity that defined "Swedishness" in Worcester was based on the following three character traits: Republican, Protestant and temperate. For the Swedes, this worked.

In simple terms, think of the dilemma ethnic groups faced in the city as such: each worried about what its ethnic rivals were doing to promote themselves as "good Americans" and worried still about how its respective community appeared to the Yankee hierarchy. People of each respective group therefore played a balancing act involved in efforts promoting themselves as non-threatening, loyal Americans to the Yankee hierarchy, yet at the same time casting a worried glance over their shoulders at their ethnic competitors to see what they were up to. Much effort went into this multifaceted identity creation.

By the late 1880s, there developed an association between Worcester's Yankee hierarchy and the Swedish-American community. In the ethnic mix that was Worcester, religion—namely Protestantism—was a common bond between these two groups. The roots of this association can be traced to an 1888 anti-liquor license meeting at Mechanics Hall; in attendance were Republican leaders and supporters. In a move that surprised organizers, about six hundred of the city's Scandinavian residents marched to the rally in support of the anti-liquor license. At this time, voters in towns and cities throughout Massachusetts decided annually whether to allow the sale of liquor within their respective communities. The liquor issue had always been controversial in Worcester, but its appearance as an annual vote on the ballot by the 1880s heightened tensions and brought the issue to the forefront. This annual vote would spark heated debates until Prohibition settled the issue on a national level.

"The Swedish people are all Protestants," stated the Swedish spokesman at Mechanics Hall. American ideals were in opposition to the sale of liquor, and as such, the American people "will find that we will not antagonize those principles."[36] The spokesman continued by advocating support for the Republican mayoral candidate. In the context of this speech, local Swedish-American leaders were letting the Yankee hierarchy know what they could expect from the Swedes and, more importantly, that the values of the Swedish-American community were synonymous to American values. In the tumultuous society of industrial Worcester, the Swedes had publicly chosen sides. The seeds of an ethnic identity in Worcester had been planted.

The Swedes entered an explosive political arena. The city's Republican Party at this time was a party divided and composed of two factions: Elite Republicans and the Citizen Coalition (a Republican-Democrat coalition). This political framework defined the political atmosphere in Worcester during the 1880s and 1890s.[37] The two factions were as follows:

Coalition Republicans

- Members of the Citizen Coalition.
- Temperate but avoided controversy with Irish Catholic constituents, many of whom had ties with the liquor trade. Coalition members consequently promoted voluntary temperance.
- Advocated the expansion of city services, which had the support of industrial and business leaders.
- Reached out to Irish Catholic Democratic constituency.

Elite Republicans

- Staunchly prohibitionist.
- Advocated for small government and low taxes. Such a stance was popular with working- and middle-class Yankees.
- Nativist in outlook. Irish monopoly of Democratic Party was perceived as a threat.

Ethnicity quickly entered the political arena. In the early 1890s, Superintendent of Schools Alfred Marble fired high school principal Alfred

Roe over his apparent discriminatory policies concerning Irish-American students. But there was more at stake than an apparent conflict within the school department. In this politically charged era, the future course of the city was seen as being in jeopardy. Marble, as with Coalition Republicans, believed that the success of the city rested on the social acceptance of all ethnic nationalities. Roe, in a vision that mirrored the Elite Republicans, acknowledged the city's diverse population but held that the Yankee Protestant formed "the foundation of New England's character, determines her purposes, and makes and maintains her reputation."[38]

Anti-Marble forces succeeded in forcing the resignation of the superintendent in 1894, but not before the ethnic and political lines had been drawn. With Swedish support, the Elite Republican faction had succeeded in not only removing the superintendent but also breaking the hold of coalition forces at city hall. The Swedes had established a solid reputation for themselves within the rank and file of the Republican Party. Such a makeup would characterize the party until the 1920s.

The seeds of a Swedish-American ethnic identity had been sown and now were bearing fruit: Worcester Swedes were Republican, Protestant and temperate. This identity was carefully maintained, especially when it came to temperance, and "all Swedes, whether wet or dry in their personal convictions, had a powerful motive to differentiate themselves from other ethnic groups, and from the Irish above all."[39] The Swedes, therefore, could be counted on standing beside the forces of Prohibition (at least publicly) when it came to voting on one of the most controversial issues of the period. The fact that a majority of churchgoers belonged to conservative, non-Lutheran and pro-temperance denominations made their stand on the issue even clearer.

The period of the 1890s to 1920s can be seen as one of political partisanship in Worcester. Within this context, the city's major ethnic groups became representative of the political parties themselves. Irish Catholics, Jews and, to a lesser extent, French-Canadians supported the Democratic Party, while the Swedes, British, English Canadians and a majority of the Yankee vote supported the Republican platform. Swedes experienced a city in flux. Ethnic, religious and political factors made for disputes among the various ethnic and social groups. The Swedes, like other groups, had to choose a side. Such political and ethnic alliances resulted in unusually placid elections. Democrats would cater to their constituents but avoid outright battles with Republican supporters, for they needed a percentage of the Yankee vote to win. Republicans, on the other hand, would also avoid outright battles since they needed a portion of the Catholic vote, usually culled from the French-Canadian community. The French-Canadians,

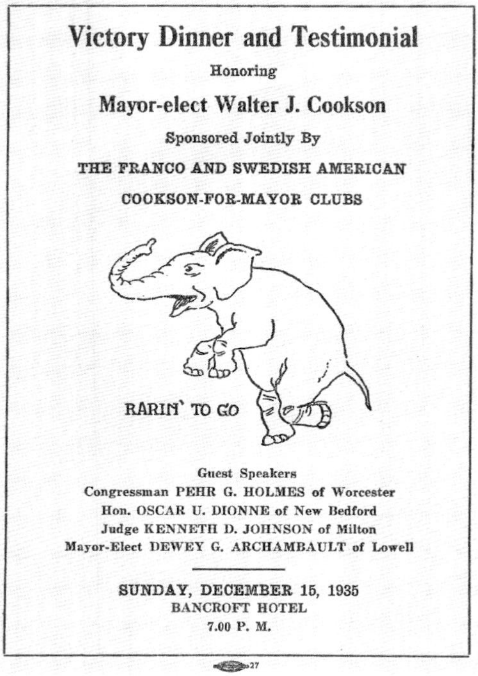

Victory Dinner and Testimonial

Honoring

Mayor-elect Walter J. Cookson

Sponsored Jointly By

THE FRANCO AND SWEDISH AMERICAN

COOKSON-FOR-MAYOR CLUBS

RARIN' TO GO

Guest Speakers

Congressman PEHR G. HOLMES of Worcester

Hon. OSCAR U. DIONNE of New Bedford

Judge KENNETH D. JOHNSON of Milton

Mayor-Elect DEWEY G. ARCHAMBAULT of Lowell

SUNDAY, DECEMBER 15, 1935

BANCROFT HOTEL

7.00 P. M.

Swedes and Franco-Americans came together to elect Walter J. Cookson mayor of Worcester in the 1935 election. Sadly, Cookson would die suddenly while attending the 1936 Republican National Convention. *Author's collection.*

in fact, were important to both parties. Although French-Canadians were inclined to vote Democratic, leaders of the Republican Party would, from time to time, play on French-Canadian fears of an Irish-dominated Catholic hierarchy in order to sway the vote. In many instances, the French-Canadians would support the Republicans should the party ticket include ethnically compatible candidates (i.e., French-Canadians).

This unusual political and ethnic atmosphere is why Worcester remained immune from the nativist hysteria that characterized the nation during the World War I era. The Swedes remained isolated from such injustices, and contrary to events that occurred nationwide, Worcester voters elected Swedish-born Pehr Holmes mayor in 1916, 1917 and 1918.

The political arena was transformed as the Republican Party, with Swedish support, ascended to political power. Between 1885 and 1919, the Republicans lost only seven of the annual mayoral races, while manufacturers or top officials of industry held the mayor's office twenty-two times between 1871 and 1920. In the other years, professionals with ties to industry were elected. Historian Roy Rosenzweig noted that "the integration of the Swedish working class into the Republican Party—an alliance forged largely through the temperance issue—goes a long way toward explaining both the local predominance of the Republican Party and the absence of mayors or other political leaders from working-class backgrounds."[40]

By the turn of the twentieth century, the Swedish-American community had skillfully created an alliance with the dominant Yankee hierarchy. This relationship benefited both groups and, in turn, led to the development of an ethnic identity based on a certain political, religious and social attributes. These attributes were to characterize the Worcester Swedes for an entire generation.

Worcester was a city in flux by 1920. The ethnic and industrial structure that had kept politics respectable was undergoing severe transformations. Immigration continued but was primarily composed of "new immigrants" from southern and eastern Europe (Italians, Poles, Lithuanians). Coinciding with the demographic change was the decline in relative numbers of the older immigrant stock (the English and the Swedes). Although naturalized in fewer numbers than their predecessors, these new immigrants nonetheless began to transform the political landscape by gravitating toward the ranks of the Democrats. In addition, national events came into play. Many immigrant groups throughout the country perceived the enactment of Prohibition and the support of immigration restriction as a personal assault instigated by the Republican national leadership. The industrial fortunes of the city began to level, and the 1920s would mark the pinnacle of industry in Worcester.

The success of the Republican effort in electing Pehr Holmes mayor (1916–18) was dampened when Democratic candidate Peter F. Sullivan, an Irish Catholic, won the election of 1919. Despite repeated Republican attempts to return a Yankee candidate to office, "Peter the Great" won reelection in 1920, 1921 and 1922. By 1923, Sullivan had become the most successful of Worcester's Irish politicians, according to several local historians.

As if "Peter the Great" wasn't enough of a threat, the 1923 election shook the Swedish-Republican alliance to its core. The party that year nominated Irish Catholic Michael J. O'Hara for mayor. The former Irish-Republican partnership of the late nineteenth century had been reestablished at the expense of the middle-class contingency that included the Swedes.

Just how the new ethnic and political developments affected the average Worcester Swede is unknown; it can be proven, however, that a large number of Worcester Swedes gravitated toward the revived Ku Klux Klan, which was then actively recruiting new members in the Northeast.

Nationally, the Klan experienced fantastic growth in the 1920s. Having been given new life in 1915, the "new Klan" focused not only on black citizens but also inculcated the fears many had of Catholics, Jews and immigrants. The Klan also promoted temperance, Protestantism, patriotism and "Americanism." In a sense, this Klan resurgence was the result of a rapidly changing American society—one that was torn between the old, traditional ways of the Victorian era and those of the new, contemporary age. The

1920s was a socially traumatic period for many, and by the middle of the decade, Klan membership had soared to more than 3 million nationwide.

In 1923, the king kleagle of the Maine Realm spoke at Mechanics Hall to kick off a membership drive, and within a year, Klan membership in the city had grown to about four thousand people. The presence of the Klan symbolized the resurgence of ethnic tensions and ethnic identity in Worcester. As historian John McClymer noted:

> *Those who joined proclaimed their Americanism. So did those who attacked them. At the same time, Swedes who joined the Klan…simultaneously proclaimed their ethnicity, as did those who opposed the KKK by joining the Knights of Columbus…Their dispute was over both the meaning of "Americanism" and over which ethnic groups were entitled to claim American nationality.*[41]

Assumption College professors John McClymer and Charles Estus have stated that for the remainder of the 1920s, ethnic tensions, particularly between the Irish and Swedish, remained volatile. Episodes of violence punctuated Klan rallies, particularly during 1924, when opponents attacked supporters in Lancaster, Spencer and Stow. A Worcester rally in Greendale on October 19 attracted a crowd of fifteen thousand. As the "Klanvocation" ended, violence broke out. Cars were burned and overturned, and people were beaten by Klan opponents. This rally remains the largest gathering of the KKK in New England.

The culmination of ethnic tensions occurred during the presidential campaign of 1928. For many in Worcester and across the nation, the choice between Republican Herbert Hoover or Democrat (and Roman Catholic) Al Smith seemed to come down to a choice between the virtuous values of a rural, old-stock Protestant America versus a decadent, urban, ethnically diverse Catholic America. On election eve, these tensions exploded in Worcester, resulting in the largest election eve riot in the United States and involving upward of twenty thousand people. Although no one was killed, there were numerous injuries. The violence of the night before carried over into election day, as Republican voters were accosted on their way to the polls; most of the violence occurred in Swedish-American enclaves.

As the period drew to a close, ethnic tensions began to subside. The Swedish-American Republicans tried unsuccessfully to regain a foothold in city politics, but their candidate, Roland S.G. Frodigh, was defeated in the 1927 and 1929 primaries. In 1931, he lost the mayoral race. Former mayor and local businessman Pehr Holmes fared better. He was elected to Congress in 1930 and served until his retirement in 1947.

The early Swedish-American ethnic identity was created out of the tumultuous political, ethnic and religious makeup in Worcester. The ethnic identity that developed out of this maelstrom defined the Swedish-American community within this context. But this context had limitations. The expectations of the Yankee hierarchy most certainly weighed heavily on the creation of a Swedish-American ethnic identity. Gary Gerstle stated that "that the nation itself, like class, gender, and race, necessarily limits the array of identities available to Americans seeking diversity."[42] Gerstle's thesis maintains that coercion played a role in the development of ethnic identities in the United States. Could coercion have played a role in the creation of the Swedish-American ethnic identity in Worcester? Earlier, it was stated that every Swede in Worcester had a powerful motive to distinguish himself from those in other ethnic groups, chief among them the Irish. It was also noted that the Swedes, in order to participate, had to choose sides. The very makeup of society in Worcester, as well as the nation, seemed to have encouraged the development of ethnic rivalries and identity creation, and the Worcester Swedes were no exception.

It is a great mistake to believe that the Swedish-American ethnic identity in Worcester ended with the 1920s. On the contrary, the idea of "Swedishness," however transformed, was kept alive through the organizational network over the course of subsequent generations. Many organizations, such as the Swedish National Federation, increased their activities during the 1940s and 1950s. Some of the lodges affiliated with the Vasa Order of America, as well, retained the Swedish language well into the 1960s, although the number of overall lodges declined. The decline in the Vasa lodges mirrored the continuous decline in the overall organizational network beginning in the 1970s and continuing unabated until the present day. Currently, the surviving organizations face obstacles, as discussed previously.

There are two wonderful sources relating to the Swedish-American community that are unpublished gems, both of them Clark University dissertations. Clergyman Karl Karlson wrote the first in 1910. In his introduction, the Worcester clergyman advised readers that his was not a history but rather a social survey of the current population. "I shall present the facts as I have found them and be as impartial as anybody possibly can," wrote Karlson, concerning his study of the "industrial, peace-loving, and law-abiding Swedish settlement."[43] Thirty-seven years later, Worcester schoolteacher Esther Wahlstrom compiled her extensive history on the community. Comparing

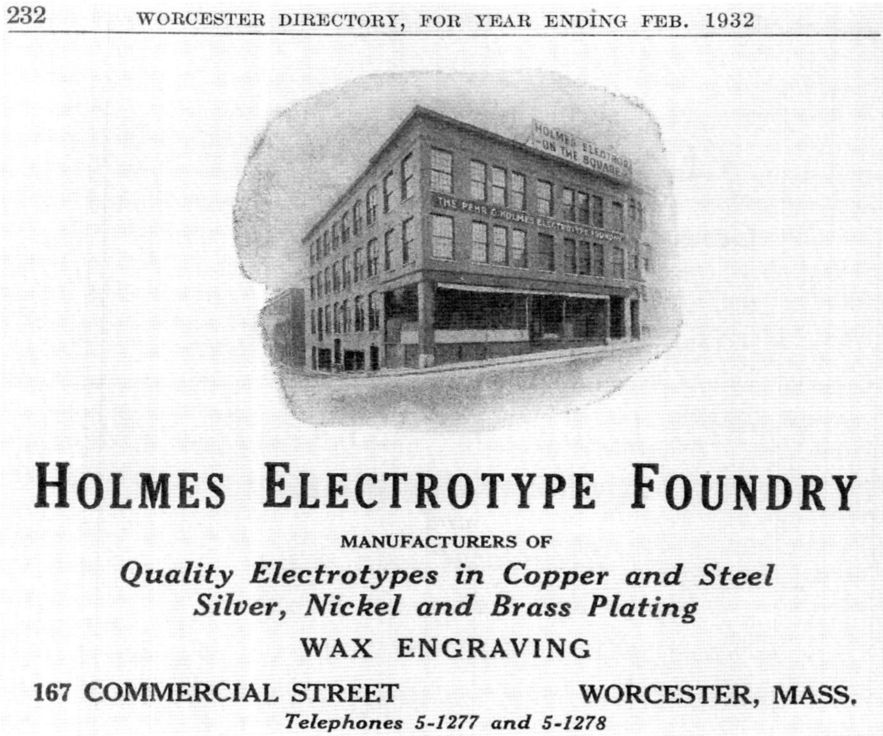

A 1931 advertisement for Holmes Electrotype, which Pehr Holmes founded in 1909. By this time, it had grown to be one of the largest businesses of its kind in New England. *Author's collection.*

both highlights the transformation of the Swedish-American community over the course of a generation, and these sources shall be referred to on numerous occasions henceforth. In addition, several related theses shall be quoted. As a group, these additional theses augment other Swedish-American accounts. At times, I will add my impressions about the present-day community in order to make this account as up to date as possible. Discussions will focus on the transformation of the Swedish-American community through selected religious institutions, industry and neighborhoods, social and fraternal organizations and benevolent organizations.

Chapter 4

IDENTITY AND GOD

The Swedish-American Churches

By the turn of the twentieth century, there had been ten Swedish-American congregations organized in the Worcester area. This number had increased to sixteen by the late 1920s as additional congregations were established in subsequent city neighborhoods and surrounding towns; some were short-lived. The spread of the Swedish congregations throughout the area was due in large part to the expansion of the mother church and subsequent development of daughter congregations. In some instances, churches established small chapels that eventually formed their own separate congregations as the membership warranted. It should be noted that many of these congregations would construct new edifices and undergo various name changes over the course of their histories. The following table has been compiled by the author of the area's original congregations.

TABLE 5. ORIGINAL SWEDISH CONGREGATIONS OF GREATER WORCESTER

Organized As	*Date*	*Original Church*
First Swedish Methodist Episcopal	1878	1884
First Swedish Congregational	1880	1885
First Swedish Baptist	1880	1884
Swedish Evangelical Lutheran Gethsemane+	1881	1882–86
Second Swedish Methodist	1885	1885 (purchased)
Swedish Christian Workers Association*	1892	1895
Saint Sigfrid's Episcopal^	1893	none

Organized As	*Date*	*Original Church*
Second Swedish Congregational	1895	1901
Swedish Evangelical Lutheran Emanuel	1896	1899
Second Swedish Baptist	1896	1897
Scandinavian Methodist Episcopal Mission^	1902	none
Scandinavian Seventh Day Adventist	1907	1908
Evangelical Lutheran Zion	1914	1916–20
Calvary Lutheran (English-speaking)+	1921	1925
Bethel Lutheran**	1924	1924–29
Swedish Pentecostal Assembly^	1926	none
Immanuel Lutheran*	1928	1929

Key: *Holden congregation **Auburn congregation
^dissolved +merged into Trinity Lutheran

Despite the popular connotation of the Swedish-American as a member of the Lutheran Church, it is apparent from this table that the first congregations organized in the Worcester area were, in fact, non-Lutheran denominations. This might be partly explained by the attitude of the Church of Sweden, which advocated that the Episcopal Church in America would be the obvious choice for Swedish Lutherans.[44] Many of the earliest Swedish Lutherans in Worcester did, in fact, worship at All Saints Episcopal Church on Pleasant Street until the organization of their own congregation. The beginnings were not easy, as support was not as forthcoming as it had been for previous Swedish congregations. Thus these early Swedish Lutherans "could not expect help from the Americans, as other Swedish denominations were being helped. The 'American' denominations could not see why the Lutherans would not join with them under their banners. What do you think would have happened if these few faithful Lutherans had not been true to the faith of their fathers?"[45]

This reference to the "faith of their fathers" illustrates how important religion was in terms of identity. For the Lutherans, as well as for the various Swedish denominations of Worcester, religion was a powerful character trait. Religion, however, could both unite and divide the community. The Swedes, for self-promotion, could unite under the Protestant banner, but the differing religious doctrines—Lutheran, Methodist, Baptist and so forth—made religious unity impossible within the confines of the Swedish-American community itself. In his study of Worcester, Roy Rosenzweig wrote of the Swedish denominations, "Such conflicts between the brännvin-drinking, card-playing Lutherans and teetotaling, Bible-reading pietists divided early nineteenth century Sweden as it would late nineteenth century Worcester."[16]

Church activities and organizations formed a community of their own. The majority of churches established religious, social, musical and athletic clubs. For example, the many groups sponsored by the First Swedish Baptist Church in 1900 included the Betesda Sunday School; a sick benefit society; the Enighet (Unity) Women's Club; a youth federation; and *Vårblomman* (May Flowers), a Sunday school subsidiary. In 1910, Karl Karlson stated that to elaborate on all of these religious organizations would be "an endless task," for "there is an endless chain of dissolution of old and formation of new."[17]

Among the more important organizations, according to Karlson, were the Sunday schools. These schools, he stated, were of the outmost importance in teaching, first, the Bible and religious fundamentals; second, good citizenship and morals; and third, the Swedish language. Karlson was passionate in dealing with the question of language preservation. The Sunday schools, he argued, must teach the Swedish language to children in order to survive, for "the parents want them to learn Swedish and therefore send them to a Sunday School that teaches Swedish." Karlson lamented, however, the fact that the teachers, most of them American-born, "have learned to speak, read and write English and use that in their everyday life and so are not able to handle Swedish as is necessary in order to impart it to the scholars." As a consequence, "there is a good deal of mixing of both languages and pure Swedish is not taught in any Sunday school."[18] As early as 1910, the beginnings of a language shift were already underway.

Of the varying denominations, Karlson paid respect to the Augustana Lutheran Synod for "the translation and spreading of the Swedish literature in the country," although he noted that "more remains to be done."[19] Karlson was correct in his compliment of the synod. At the time Karlson was composing his dissertation, the synod's publishing house, the Augustana Book Concern (ABC), was the largest of the Swedish-American publishing concerns in the country, with branch bookstores in Rock Island, Illinois; St. Paul, Minnesota; New York City; and Chicago. The ABC was also the most prominent importer of Swedish-language publications in the United States.

By the second decade of the twentieth century, however, these great bastions of Swedish language preservation had largely given themselves over to the English language. "Achieving oral and written fluency among second-generation immigrants is always an elusive goal, for a language can easily become stilted and cease to evolve when the community speaking it is separated from their country of origin." So wrote the historian of Salem

MINNES-ALBUM
FÖRSTA LUTHERSKA KYRKAN
WORCESTER, MASSACHUSETTS

Med kort historik över församlingen och hennes verksamhetsgrenar

UTGIVEN MED ANLEDNING AV FYRTIOFEM-ÅRSFESTEN DEN 21-24 OKTOBER, 1926

"Sällt är det folk som förstår jubelklangen!
Herre, i ditt ansiktes ljus skola de vandra."
Ps. 89: 16.

The forty-fifth-anniversary booklet of the First Lutheran Church from 1926. Five years later, the commemorative fifty-year history was written largely in English. *Author's collection.*

Covenant (First Swedish Congregational) Church in 1980, in retrospect on the loss of the church's Swedish-language Sunday school around World War I.[50] A decade after the loss of the Congregational Sunday school, a history of the First Swedish Baptist Church noted that one of "the biggest problems" concerning their respective Sunday school was "the language question." In 1930, as this Baptist history was being written, the generational shift was such that it was noted "at the present time, English is used almost entirely."[51]

This shift toward the use of the English language was not confined to the Sunday schools. Religious services were slowly being transformed as the use of English increased. At the Swedish Evangelical Lutheran Emanuel Church in Quinsigamond Village, English services had been conducted on an infrequent basis beginning as early as 1915. When the thirty-five-year history of the church was written in 1931, however, it noted that the issue of language had never been problematic at the church. By this time, Emanuel was offering English services on the second Sunday afternoon and the fourth Sunday evening. It was noted that to conduct these services 150 new English-language hymnals had to be ordered.

The experiences of the ethnic churches in dealing with the so-called language question illustrate a community in flux. At First Swedish Congregational, the use of English twice a month had taken place by 1928, although Swedish services continued on a regular basis until the 1940s. The practice of retaining some Swedish services here continued late into that decade, for in 1947, Esther Wahlstrom noted that the church was one of the last to do so. Despite such efforts, Congregational church leaders bowed to the inevitable. The pastor, fluent in Swedish, "reluctantly" issued his 1939 annual report to the church in English, and subsequently, the 1938 annual report was "the last in the mother tongue" of church founders.[52]

At First Lutheran Church, the transition to English was seen as a foregone conclusion. The fifty-year history, largely published in English in 1931, noted, "Up to this time our Sunday morning services have as a general rule been conducted in the Swedish language. But times have changed. Immigration has been practically stopped. Therefore, the time will soon come, when we will find it expedient to have one or two Sunday morning services each month in the American language."[53]

Bethlehem Evangelical (Second Swedish Congregational) Church went over to all-English services by 1938; four years later, the First Swedish Baptist Church followed suit. In 1927, Bethel Lutheran Church in Auburn was using both Swedish and English on an alternating weekend schedule, and by 1929, the English services were attracting more congregants on

Left: During the pastorate of Anders Gottfrid Lund (1928–45), Bethlehem Evangelical Church weathered the Great Depression and World War II and transitioned to all-English services. *Author's collection.*

Below: The establishment of Calvary Lutheran Church, seen here circa 1949, represented continuing shifts within the ethnic community in terms of language and religion. *Author's collection.*

average. By 1941, the use of Swedish had been relegated to one Sunday a month, a practice that effectively continued until 1945. Similarly, at Swedish Methodist Church as late as 1945, services were conducted in Swedish once a month. This practice, however, ended the following year. So rapidly had the transformation to English been that in 1947, Esther Wahlstrom would write, "The Swedish churches of Worcester are growing, active churches, supported by young and old alike. Of course, there are many changes that have come with the years. There is, for instance, the disappearance of the Swedish language. This, by the way, still gives rise to many a debate among interested members of the churches."[54]

The formation in 1921 of the Calvary Lutheran congregation best illustrates the shifts within the Swedish community at the time. This congregation was established as the result of a survey undertaken to determine whether an all-English-speaking Lutheran congregation was desired in the city. On February 20, 1928, the *Evening Gazette* reported, "Seventeen nationalities are represented in the membership…this parish is entitled to be called Worcester's ecclesiastical melting pot." This great mix and steady growth of the church was credited to "the young people who know only the language of this country."

Coinciding with the language transformation was a tendency of the congregations to "mainstream" their names, with some congregations adopting banal replacements. In 1917, the Swedish Evangelical Lutheran Gethsemane Church became First Lutheran for what church fathers called "practical reasons." In 1962, Evald Benjamin Lawson, president of Upsala University in New Jersey, remarked that almost 10 percent of the Augustana churches had chosen this generic namesake. "There is no 'Second Lutheran Church' among us," Lawson retorted, "It spread almost like the measles, the change-over…two and three decades ago…Nowadays we do better than to look at the number table to select a church name. The rush to be first has subsided."[55]

In Worcester, the transition continued. The Second Swedish Congregational Church became Bethlehem Evangelical as early as March 1924, but it would take another two decades for other churches to follow suit in an attempt to expand their congregations. Epworth Swedish Methodist Church dropped "Swedish" from its official name in 1941. Two years later, First Swedish Baptist adopted the generic Belmont Street Baptist as the congregation's new name. Out in Holden, the Scandinavian Evangelical Congregational Church became simply Chaffins Congregational Church in 1947. That same year, Bethlehem Evangelical became Bethlehem Covenant Church.

Epworth Methodist Church

SALISBURY AND LANCASTER STREETS
WORCESTER, MASSACHUSETTS

Ivar F. Pearson, Minister
10 DEAN STREET
TELEPHONES: PASTOR'S RESIDENCE, 4-1041; CHURCH OFFICE, 2-2376

Verner Nelson, Organist and Director of Music
23 BARBER AVENUE

HERBERT BORG, Secretary Official Board
MISS ESTHER CARLSON, Financial Secretary
LAWRENCE S. PETERSON, Treasurer
ALBERT HORBERG, Treas. Building Fund
C. A. HORBERG, Treas. World Service Funds
GUSTAF R. NYGREN, Sexton

The Epworth congregation dropped the word "Swedish" from its name, as illustrated in this bulletin from November 22, 1942. *Author's collection.*

The various religious conferences were transforming themselves as well. The Eastern Swedish Methodist Conference of New England merged with the English-language conference in 1941, while in 1945 the Swedish Baptist General Conference acknowledged that the generational shift had so transformed the conference that the word "Swedish" was dropped out of necessity. By this time, the transition to all-English services had been completed within its member churches.

As for the Augustana Synod, the Swedish branch of the Lutheran Church in the United States had maintained a New England Conference since 1912. Fifty years later, in 1962, the Augustana Synod ceased as a separate entity and merged with various synods to form the Lutheran Church in America. The dissolution of Augustana was a landmark event in Swedish-American circles, for the synod had at one time been admired as the great preserver of the Swedish-American identity in America.

Despite the transition toward a more mainstream, "American" character, the ethnic affiliation did not completely disappear at first. The underlying ethnicity of the Lutheran congregations was highlighted in a series of special celebrations in 1948. On Sunday, May 23, Swedish Archbishop Erling Eidem officiated over two events that symbolized the connections between Worcester and Sweden. Early that day, the archbishop participated in groundbreaking ceremonies marking the construction of the Zion Lutheran Church parish house in Greendale. Afterward, the Swedish prelate participated in the dedication of a unique altar cloth made specifically for Trinity Lutheran Church by Swedish monarch Gustav V. Adolph. Hand-embroidered, the frontal is significant, for it represents one of three frontals created by the king for a church in the United States. In his remarks, Archbishop Eidem praised the immigrant generation and their descendants. "Bonds of common origin bind us together," remarked the archbishop, "I hope that these will never be broken."[56]

Perhaps unknowingly, the archbishop was continuing a tradition of religious visitations that had begun following the visit of Paul Peter Waldenström, the charismatic Swedish religious personality who lectured at Mechanics Hall in June 1889; he wrote of his experiences, "It was rightly moving," as he rekindled ties with "friends from Stockholm and some others from Göteborg…Tears were in many eyes, and I myself was choked up."[57] On Thanksgiving Day 1923, the noteworthy Swedish archbishop Nathan Söderblom paid his respects to countrymen in the city, lecturing at Clark University and First Lutheran Church and touring the Swedish Lutheran Old People's Home.

Five years later, in February 1928, the Swedish prelate was the recipient of a telephone call from *Telegram and Gazette* editor George Booth and Pastor John Eckstrom of the First Lutheran Church. The conversation between the men was significant, for this call inaugurated regular commercial telephone service between the United States and Sweden. During this historic communication on February 20, the *Worcester Telegram* reported that Booth addressed Söderblom, "I consider it a great privilege to establish this

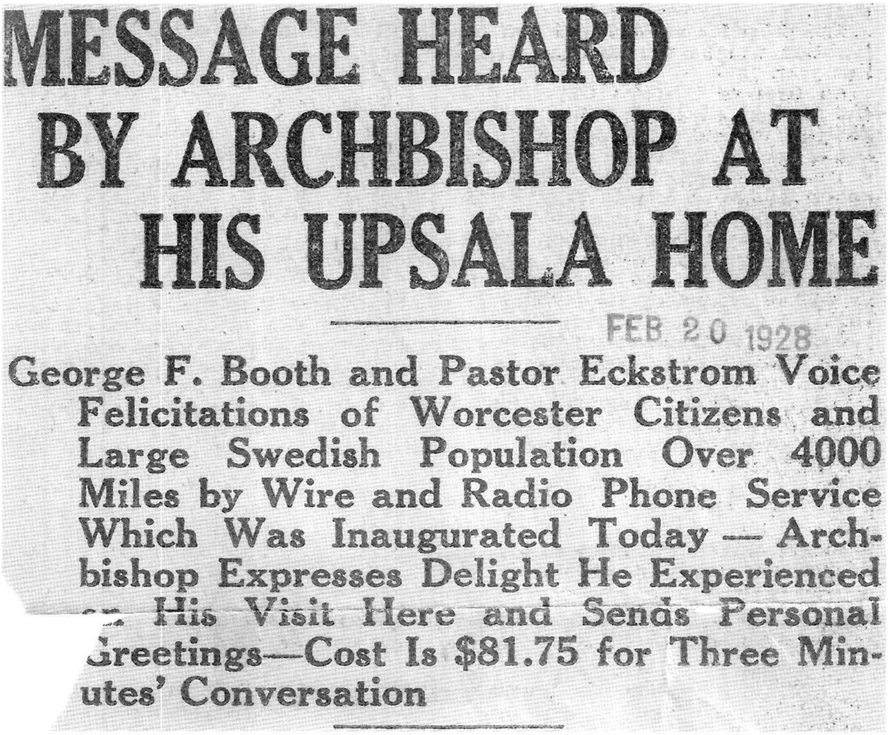

MESSAGE HEARD BY ARCHBISHOP AT HIS UPSALA HOME

FEB 20 1928

George F. Booth and Pastor Eckstrom Voice Felicitations of Worcester Citizens and Large Swedish Population Over 4000 Miles by Wire and Radio Phone Service Which Was Inaugurated Today — Archbishop Expresses Delight He Experienced on His Visit Here and Sends Personal Greetings—Cost Is $81.75 for Three Minutes' Conversation

Archbishop Söderblom sent his "greetings from the homeland" and recalled "with pleasure" his 1923 visit to Worcester during the 1928 phone call. *Author's collection.*

telephone connection…By this means we are provided the opportunity to communicate to you the greetings of the thousands of good citizens of Worcester who proudly boast that Sweden is their native land, while proclaiming their loyalty to America, the land of their adoption." This was no call for the faint of heart, as it came with an astronomical price tag: $81.75 for three minutes!

The visits of Swedish clergy occurred as recently as 1993. In November, the archbishop of Stockholm, Henrik Svenungsson, preached at Trinity Lutheran in conjunction with the 1993 *gå till Amerika* exhibit at the Worcester Historical Museum. Premiering in October of that year and running for five months, this historical exhibit celebrated 125 years of the Swedish-American presence in Worcester and gave rise to a book of the same name.

Religious ties have always been an important part of the maintenance and preservation of an ethnic identity for the majority of immigrant groups. For Worcester's Swedish-Americans, it has been shown that their Protestantism

Trinity was established as a Lutheran congregation within an American context. Nevertheless, the Swedish-inspired architecture mirrors the ethnic roots of the congregation. *Author's collection.*

tied them to the dominant Yankee hierarchy, thus providing a key ingredient to their emerging ethnic identity. The individual churches, with their amalgam of organizations, helped to fuse their respective congregations together under the Protestant banner. This banner celebrated religious as well as ethnic aspects. As the ethnic ties that bound the congregations together began to weaken over the generations, so, too, did the sense of community in a religious sense. As one local resident, Jon Lundstrom, recalled, "My father liked the social aspect of belonging to the church, and I was friends with the pastor's son…It was a social connection, not a religious one."

A dramatic ethno-religious shift took place in January 1948 with the formation of Trinity Lutheran Church. Trinity was born out of the merger between three Worcester Lutheran congregations: First (Swedish), Bethany (Swedish-Finnish) and Calvary (English-speaking). In this respect, Trinity became the realization of what had begun with the formation of Calvary Lutheran Church just two decades earlier. A 1948 copy of the *Trinity News* announcing the merger stated that among the reasons for the merger was the "realization of the fact that linguistic distinctions were rapidly becoming a thing of the past." John Jeppson, prominent Swedish-American businessman, supported this fact, noting "by 1944 English was the predominant language spoken"; he added that as a result of subsequent demographic and social changes, "membership was beginning to decline" in all three churches.[58] Consequently, the formation of an *American* Lutheran church, comprising former ethnic congregations, occurred with the construction of a new edifice beginning in 1950. However Americanized Trinity is now in membership, the church mirrors the ethnicity of its founders. So striking is the Swedish-inspired design that Trinity has been referred to by historian H. Arnold Barton as "probably the most faithful replica of traditional Swedish church architecture to be found in America."

The decline in the Protestant-ethnic facet can also be illustrated by the foundation of St. Catherine of Sweden Roman Catholic Church in 1952. Established in the Quinsigamond Village neighborhood, its very existence would have been considered an anathema in the previous generation. The establishment of a Roman Catholic parish in what was still the chief Swedish-American enclave definitely raised some eyebrows, and according to Reverend Pat Hawthorne of the Worcester Diocese, the naming of the church was undoubtedly a way to calm local concerns. By this time, the subsequent generations of Swedish-Americans had already begun to marry outside of their ethnic group—and their Protestant religion—as well.

The Protestantism that highlighted the Swedish-American ethnic identity throughout the late nineteenth century through the 1920s was thus transformed during the immediate postwar period and became less of an identifying trait as it had been previously. The resulting loss of the Swedish language within the congregations also played a major role in the decline of the church as a purely ethnic institution in Swedish Worcester. The language dilemma was not unique to the Swedish congregations. In 1934, the Norwegian Lutheran Church on Highland Street in Worcester adopted English as the official language of the church after numerous attempts to preserve the Norwegian language failed. Coinciding with the decline of the mother tongue were the generational changes that occurred. Those born and raised within the American context developed differing attitudes and ideals. This was a common occurrence among all subsequent ethnic generations. Common public schooling and popular culture did much to shape that generation into Americans who happened to be of Swedish heritage. Such transformations within these generations quickened during World War II and in postwar America, as both the unifying experience of war and subsequent exodus to surrounding towns began. For some ethnic congregations, this proved the unraveling of the congregation itself. Consider the previously mentioned Norwegian Lutheran Church. By 1975, "dispersal of church members to the suburbs and assimilation of the Norwegian community" were being cited by the pastor as factors that "took away the basic points of identity of the congregation."[59] As a consequence, the congregation was forced to disband.

The membership in area churches should also be considered. Karl Karlson noted a lack of religious interest in the 1910 Worcester community as well. "Consequently only about one fifth of the whole Swedish population is concerned in active religious work," he noted. On these low figures, he wrote, "It seems as if they left their religion behind them when they came over to this country disgusted with it." Karlson blamed the rigid structure of the State Church of Sweden, where citizens were born Lutheran and forced to support the church as a matter of policy. As such, "when they finally landed where they did not need to do it if they did not want to, they severed all connections with the church life." However, Karlson did note that those who were devoted members of area churches sacrificed much so that their churches would continue on. Many carried their faith with them throughout their lives. Mayor Andrew B. Holmstrom credited his value system with "the happy, industrious home of my Swedish-born parents, in whose lives abiding religious faith was a dominant factor. They brought me to church early and regularly."[60] It is no wonder that Holmstrom was long an officer of the Worcester Swedish Charitable Association.

It can be deduced that even though the Protestant identity was used as an early marker of Swedish-American ethnicity, well over half of the community remained outside any church. This may explain why the decline in the relative importance of the church as an ethnic institution took place within the community. In addition, the Swedish-American population, as has been discussed, were members of several contrasting religious denominations that did much to create factions within the community itself.

In comparison, the strong affiliation between the Catholic Church and Irish immigrants can be traced back to British repression and attempts to

Anglicize the population of Ireland. During this period, many areas of the nation tenaciously clung to their beliefs, and Catholicism became a quasi-nationalistic marker to those Irish Catholics. This belief was transplanted in America during the Irish immigration of the 1840s. This Irish Catholic identity was (and is) so pronounced that the Irish supported the establishment of Columbus Day during the 1890s for religious rather than ethnic reasons. Additionally, the Knights of Columbus was organized as a predominantly Irish-American organization along a Catholic, rather than Irish, identity.

Despite the changes that have occurred within the congregations over the last seventy years, there are vestiges of a Swedish-American heritage that remain. In October 2003, Trinity Lutheran, Salem Covenant and Zion Lutheran Churches participated in a three-day symposium that honored the city's Swedish past. That December, Zion Lutheran Church hosted a Julotta (early morning Christmas) service during which a mix of both Swedish and English was heard. Currently, this sacred tradition has continued, most notably at Bethel Lutheran in Auburn, Massachusetts.

The reality is, however, that the Swedish-organized churches in Worcester have been transformed from purely ethnic institutions into American denominations. Many of these churches have taken on a new ethnic dynamic all their own. For example, Kenyan immigrants have made Quinsigamond Methodist Church their place of worship in recent years. Hence, the former immigrant churches are now themselves welcoming modern-day immigrants and their children. In this respect, the transformation has come full circle.

Chapter 5

INDUSTRY AND THE SWEDISH-AMERICAN NEIGHBORHOODS

By the time Karl Karlson wrote his dissertation at Clark University in 1910, the Swedish-American community had become firmly established within the Worcester area. As we have seen, an extensive network of churches had been organized, representing an array of denominations, each with its own network. In addition, numerous businesses and industrial establishments were started, serving Worcester-area Swedes and non-Swedes alike. Many industries in Worcester spawned Swedish-American neighborhoods; the prominent enclaves shall be discussed.

Swedish-American entrepreneurs established a network of businesses throughout the city, highlighted by the establishment of the first large concern, the Swedish Mercantile Co-Op Company, in 1883. The 1896 *Svensk-Amerikanska Affärs Kalendern* lists an estimated fifty-five Swedish-run establishments within Worcester that served the expanding community. The businesses represented an array of goods and services including electrical supplies, tailoring services, musical instruments, groceries, building contracting, undertaking, home furnishings, pharmaceutical supplies and publishing. Karlson noted in 1910, "To enumerate all the Swedish business enterprices [*sic*] in Worcester would be almost impossible. A thrifty and energetic people that does not give up what it has undertaken for anything that comes along will always find outlet for its energy. And so one store after another has risen as sponges from moist ground and flourished."

But it was in the industrial sphere that the Swedish-American community prospered. Longtime concerns included Hollander and Johnson, Lundquist

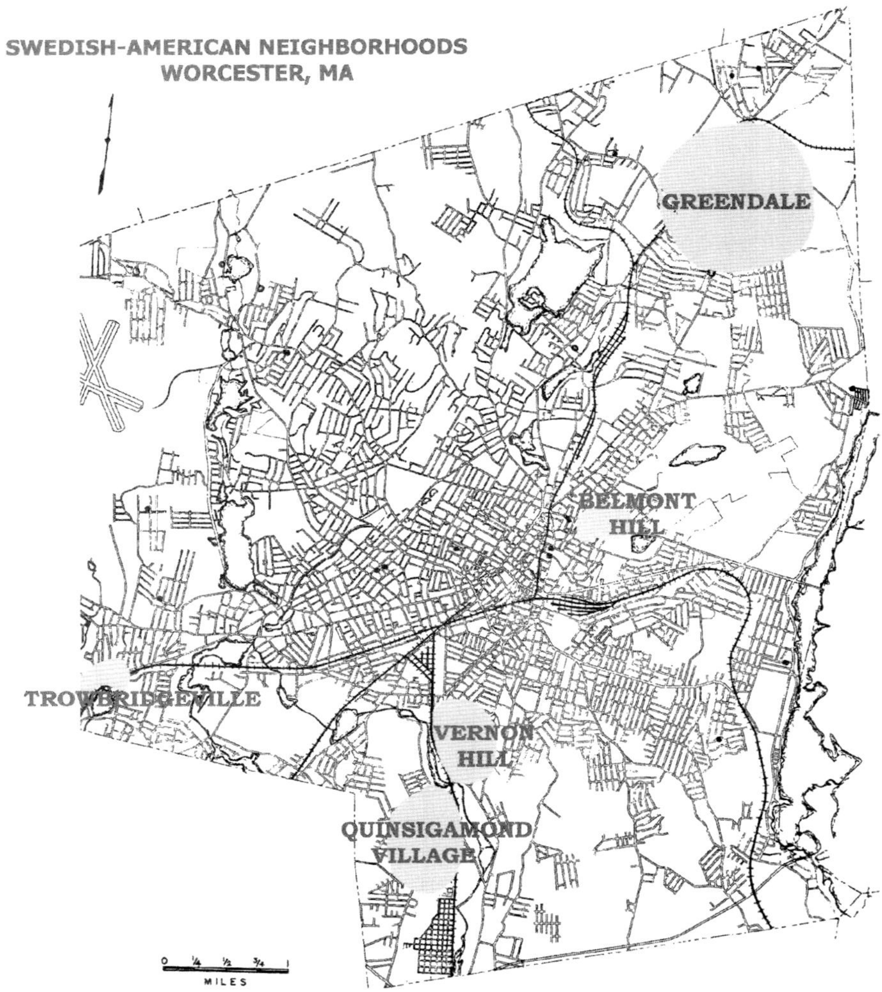

This map highlights the primary Swedish neighborhoods of Worcester. With the exception of Trowbridgeville, all were located in proximity to major industries. *Author's collection.*

Tool and Manufacturing, Olson Manufacturing, Johnson Steel and Wire, and Holmes Electrotype. A few, such as Worcester Tool and Stamping and Paramount Oilless Bearing Company (POBCO), survive to this day. Among the largest of the industries in Worcester was the Norton Company, located in the Greendale section of the city. Under the reign of the early superintendent, Höganäs-born John Jeppson, the abrasive complex became a destination for thousands of area Swedes. By 1900,

Birthday greetings from Worcester to Höganäs, 1911. *Author's collection.*

more than half of the workforce was Swedish, with natives from Jeppson's hometown constituting the majority.

Migration from Höganäs to Worcester is classic chain migration. Höganäs historian Brita Hardenby remembered, "*Det har berättats för mig att när resandet var som livligast mellan Höganäs och Worcester då räckte det med att säga att den och den skulle 'gå till Jeppsons shop.' Alla visste precis vad det betydde. Nu skulle ännu en familj flytta till Amerika.*" ("It was told to me that when travel was at it heaviest between Höganäs and Worcester that it was enough to say 'go to Jeppson's shop.' All knew precisely what it meant. Now another family shall move to America.")[61]

Visiting Swedish researcher Helge Nelson noted of Greendale, "Swedes and descendants of Swedes constitute the majority in several blocks…due to the large grinding and emery manufactories of the Norton Company." He went on to state that Norton's was still called "*Höganäs-shopet* in good Swedish-American vernacular." A Höganäs Society was organized in 1904 and remained active well into the 1960s. As late as 1925, Nelson estimated that no less than 50 percent of the workforce was of Swedish descent.

Jeppson was instrumental in the establishment of the Indian Hill development, created by the Norton Company exclusively for Norton employees, the great majority being Swedes. By 1920, this prime example of corporate paternalism had attracted nationwide attention, being noted for its layout, designed by prominent architect Grosvenor Atterbury. In 1916, former president Theodore Roosevelt, himself an advocate of planned housing, paid the development a visit and planted a ceremonial oak that stands to this day at the corner of Indian Hill and Poniken Roads. Charles G. Washburn noted in *Industrial Worcester* that the entire community was one of "the most suggestive and promising" of any Worcester neighborhood: "It is planned for utility, economy, and beauty." Inspiration for such housing came from Jeppson's roots, remembering the workers' housing of his native Höganäs. As late as 1947, Wahlstrom remarked, "Almost every house in this attractive settlement has a nameplate that is Swedish."

For decades, the Norton Company sponsored an array of activities for its employees: bowling, crew, tennis and other sports; a stamp club; a camera club; and various social clubs. The company maintained a field house and private beach along the shores of Indian Lake for the enjoyment of its employees. A visiting nurse and credit union were additional benefits that employees appreciated. The *Norton Spirit* was a popular weekly publication that kept employees "in the loop" as to what was going on in and around the various plants. One of the largest company expansions came in 1953 with the construction of a million-dollar Machine Tool Division on Brooks Street.

The Jeppson name became legendary in Worcester and one noted for its benevolence, both within the Swedish-American community and beyond. The family was instrumental in the development and expansion of the

"2,550 hrs, 12,633 ft. Pine." Swedish-Americans Norman Grahn and Thurston Solomon, pattern makers in the Machine Tool Division, pose with their handiwork for the proposed Boeing SST supersonic jet in 1967. *Author's collection.*

Swedish Lutheran Old People's Home and a chapel at both Zion Lutheran and Trinity Lutheran Churches, while the family home at 1 Drury Lane was gifted to WPI in 1941 and has since been used as the home of the college president. Son George and grandson John II carried on the family tradition of community service.

Norton was one of the primary industrial centers that attracted Swedes, another being the previously mentioned American Steel and Wire complexes. By 1915, a quarter of the workforce at its Southworks plant was of Swedish descent. The earliest Swedish-American center developed around this complex as early as the 1870s, when Swedish Methodists from Ishpeming, Michigan, arrived in the city. By the turn of the twentieth century, the Swedish presence was firmly established in Quinsigamond Village, south of the city center. Few ethnic enclaves "were so homogenous…The Village was unusual not just for Worcester, but for the U.S. as a whole."[62] Indeed, it has been estimated that at one time the percentage of Swedes living in the Village was well over 70 percent. Thoroughfares in "the Village" today validate the Swedish legacy: Stockholm, Halmstad, Eckman, Carlstad, Dybeck, Forsberg and Kosta Streets. In 1902, visiting Swedish commentator Carl Sundbeck toured Swedish-American centers throughout the country and gave the following account of Quinsigamond Village (translation by author):

> *Et litet stycke söder om staden ligger en ännu store koloni, mest bestående af värmlänningar och andra bergslagsbor. Det är Washburn and Moen Mfg. Co:s stora stålverk, numera en del af U.S. Steel corporation. Platsens namn är Quinsigamond. Men i staden med detta besynnerliga namn heter gatorna Halmstads- Ekmans- och Karlstadsgatan! Och vid dessa gator ligga små vänliga trähus, innehållande från tre till sex rum hvardera. Det är svensk-amerikanska arbetares hem, och har framlefva de sitt lif.*[63]

> [A little south of the city lies yet another large colony, mostly consisting of people from Värmland and other people living in Bergslagen. There is Washburn and Moen Manufacturing Company's large steel works, now a part of U.S. Steel Corporation. The name of the place is Quinsigamond. But in the town with the strange name are streets named Halmstad- Ekman- and Karlstad streets! And on those streets lie small, friendly wooden houses, consisting of three to six rooms each. They are Swedish-American worker's homes, and here they are living their lives.]

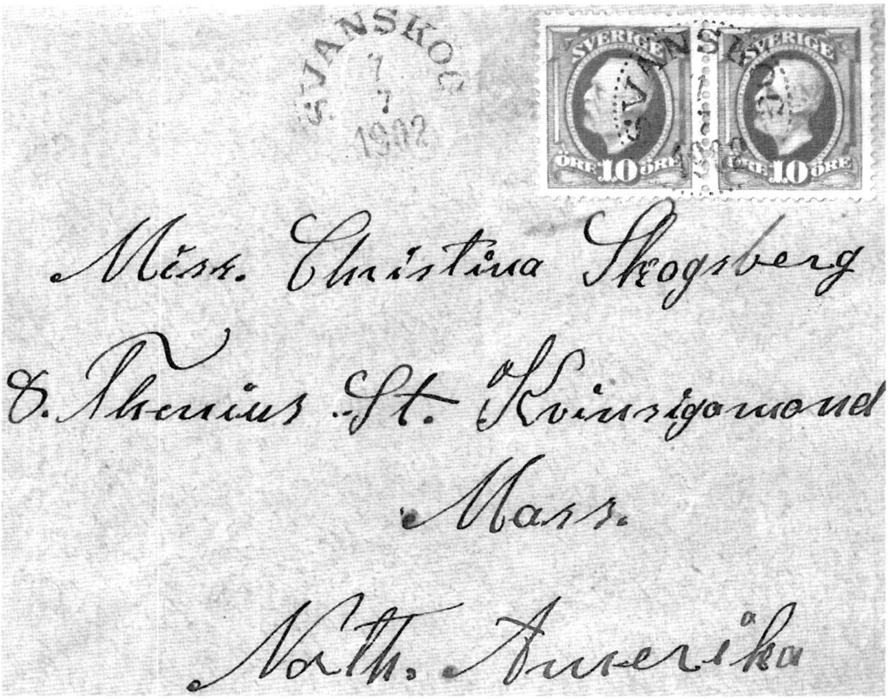

Letter from Svanskog, Sweden, to Christina Skogsberg, 1902. Letters were often addressed to Quinsigamond, not Worcester, Massachusetts. Note the Swedish phonetic spelling "Kvinsigamond." *Author's collection.*

Unlike the several other Swedish-American neighborhoods, Quinsigamond Village took on an identity of its own. The Village was the only neighborhood to have its own associated organizations. There was the Quinsigamonds Väl Lodge IOGT, Quinsigamond Lodge VOA and the Quinsigamond Athletic Club. For generations, Quinsigamond was synonymous with Swedish. The 1939 South High yearbook, for example, described senior Helen Werme as "one of those blond, blue-eyed girls from Quinsigamond Village." Although the description failed to mention her ethnic heritage, her very characteristics and locality implied that fact.

Another Swedish-American neighborhood was established around the Southworks complex on the upper slopes of neighboring Vernon Hill. Although considered a part of Quinsigamond Village by some researchers, this community was a separate entity in many ways. A neighborhood school was located here, as was the Second Swedish Baptist Church on Harlem Street. As in the Village, street names today bear the mark of these early

Helen E. Werme

Do you hear all that noise and giggles from that group of girls? Yes, you're right! Helen is in the middle of it. She is one of those blond, blue-eyed girls from Quinsigamond Village. She is in the Senior Choir and the Vagabonds Club is much more lively with her presence. Helen is always ready to help her friends and laugh them out of their worries. She plans to go in training at City Hospital next fall and we wish the future nurse all the luck in the world.

Girls' Glee Club 2, 3, 4 Girl Reserves 3, 4 Vagabonds 4
Philomathea 3, 4 Senior Choir 3, 4
French Club 4 Basketball 3, 4

Helen Werme's 1939 yearbook description epitomized the view many in the Worcester area had about Quinsigamond Village and its residents. *Author's collection.*

Swedish residents. Upsala Street, Svea Street, Lund Street and Koping (in Swedish *Köping*) Street are found in proximity of one another. Harold Creveling, in his 1951 thesis, noted "a smaller Swedish area" in the area of Vernon Hill, remarking, "the Swedes, in the latter area, are less predominant than formerly but still maintain a church."

The American Steel and Wire Northworks complex on Grove Street resulted in the establishment of a Swedish-American neighborhood within the vicinity of Belmont Hill. The area, however, was not only Swedish, as a sizeable Finnish-American community was established here as well, complete with its own religious institutions, businesses and societies. As a general rule, the Swedes settled in neighborhoods at the peak of the hill, while a majority of the Finns settled the surrounding sections such as those in the Clayton/Laurel/Prospect Street area. A smaller portion of the Nordic population was composed of Swede-Finns—ethnic Swedes from Finland who emigrated from the Swedish-speaking districts of Finland, primarily Österbotten. Considering themselves a distinct ethnic group, they established their own organizations and a church as well. As a result, the Belmont Hill neighborhoods became a mosaic of various Nordic groups, each with its own organizational and religious makeup.

As early as 1900, the Swedes had established themselves on Belmont Hill, living within the clusters of three-deckers that had come to characterize the expanding industrial city. This was the only inner-city Swedish-American enclave established, as all others were located on the city's periphery. Partly as a result, it was one of the first to dissipate. As early as 1925, Helge Nelson noted "the close Swedish settlement is being broken up" in the Belmont Hill neighborhoods, due primarily to "the exodus of the Swedes to suburban areas, where they build their own nice homes." If Nelson is accurate, then the beginning of a Swedish departure from the Belmont Hill area coincided with that of the Finns, as many from this ethnic community settled in the surrounding towns, with several establishing farms throughout the county as early as the 1910s. Wahlstrom also noted that by 1947, Belmont Hill, once known as "Scandinavian Heights," was "no longer Scandinavian but has witnessed the distribution of Swedes to other districts." Certain landmarks, however, such as the Scandinavian Salvation Army Tabernacle on Belmont Street and adjacent summer campgrounds at the corner of Olga Avenue and Vinson Street, were still quite active at the time of Wahlstrom's thesis, while First Lutheran Church remained one of the premier Swedish-American congregations. The construction of Interstate 290 in the late 1950s would dramatically alter both the physical and ethnic landscape of the Belmont Hill neighborhoods.

Researchers and historians have largely overlooked the small Swedish enclave in the city's Trowbridgeville (Hadwen Park) section, an enclave that should be considered on the list of Swedish settlements. The Swedish population was large enough to warrant the establishment of a nondenominational Swedish Sunday school by 1914. One undocumented article that year stated the school included 119 children representing five denominations in fourteen classes. This school was maintained until the mid-1930s, when recruitment efforts from neighboring Bethel Lutheran Church in Auburn resulted in the suspension of these classes. It is interesting to note that Harold Creveling perceptively included this neighborhood in his study of Worcester's ethnic groups. "A smaller area, predominantly Swedish," he wrote, "is located at Trowbridgeville in the southwestern part of Worcester beside Leesville Pond. The section is not densely built up with multi-family dwellings as is Belmont Hill, parts of Greendale, and Quinsigamond Village." Despite its rather remote location, no organized Swedish church was established, and most residents commuted to services in Worcester or to neighboring Bethel Lutheran in Auburn. Many joined the neighborhood Congregational church as well. The location of this enclave far from the industrialized areas of Worcester may be one reason why these Swedes have been largely overlooked.

It was within the industrial framework that the Swedes thrived. Karlson wrote in 1910, "The Swedish people is [*sic*] primarily an industrial people." Indeed, Nelson paid tribute to this fact in 1943. "It may be stated without exaggerating," he remarked, "that the Swedes enjoy in a higher degree than any other people the reputation of being mechanics…The Swedes thus have a respected position in the industry of Worcester." These industrial centers were the catalyst that provided the Swedes with employment opportunities,

This 1905 postcard to Sweden of the American Steel Southworks plant reads, in part, "this is part of the place Carl works in." *Author's collection.*

and in the process, they developed the skills to not only succeed but also create ethnic communities centered on several of their largest employers. Thus ethnicity, social status and occupations were factors in the development of immigrant neighborhoods.

The era of industrial development began to peak in the 1920s, although the diversified Worcester industrial base did not decline as rapidly as it did in one-industry towns such as Lowell or Haverhill. A transition in living conditions affected the city as well, particularly in the post–World War II era. For example, the Worcester School Department closed several schools within the downtown core, a result of a 1949 Columbia University study that predicted the eventual decline of inner-city living. New city schools, the report recommended, should be constructed in the northern periphery (e.g., Greendale and West Mountain Street), as those sections were developing into areas that offered better living conditions. As many inner-city neighborhoods began to show their age, they declined in relative importance as places to live, and many were transformed into "a mass of blighted homes and buildings that are no longer attractive places to live. As people become more prosperous they seek better living conditions."[64] The older Swedish-American neighborhoods therefore began to experience a decline as second- and third-generation Swedish-Americans began the transition to suburban life.

No longer needing the ethnic community for support and confident of their American identity, many left for a life outside the "old neighborhood." The most rapid decline occurred at Belmont Hill, where the transition had begun as early as the 1920s. In Quinsigamond Village, Harold Creveling noted this transition in 1951. Although he acknowledged that "Swedish group consciousness" was still strong within the Village, he noted that a population shift was underway: "It is apparent that the older and more predominantly Scandinavian sections such as Quinsigamond and Belmont Hill were less desirable, from a residential point of view, than those farther from industrial areas." Consequently, as subsequent generations of Swedish-Americans became more affluent, "they sought homes in more desirable places that were less crowded." Journalist Ellis I. Folke, who had visited the city in 1949, noted the speed of the overall assimilation process in Worcester by 1958:

> *It is true that you still run into an unusual number of Johanssons, Carlssons, and Petterssons in the Worcester telephone book, that there is a Swedish-language newspaper, that there are several Swedish fraternal, religious, and other organizations. But to call Worcester a "Swedish community" obviously would be wrong. With a speed that is rather amazing, the Swedes in Worcester, admittedly a large national group, are being assimilated into the general population…the Worcester Swedes not only follow a pattern that is typical…but are actually advancing ahead of it.*[65]

A January 31, 1971 *Sunday Telegram* article highlighted the transformation of the Village. "A lot of the old Swedes have left," remarked one resident, while another lamented, "Today you don't hear much Swedish spoken in the Village." Did the ethnic neighborhood contain the seeds of its own dissolution? Were not these neighborhoods designed to support and promote the social mobility and acculturation of its residents into the dominant American culture? This seems to ring true for the Swedish-Americans of Worcester, but the dissolution of the ethnic neighborhoods did not necessarily mean the end of the community. In this respect, I take issue with Folke's perception of what a "community" constitutes. That Worcester as a city was not a "Swedish community" is true, but the Swedes as an ethnic group were certainly still strong. The ethnic community, as discussed, has transcended the bounds of physical boundaries characterized by simple neighborhoods and organizations.

Presently, there is hope that Quinsigamond Village will undergo a transformation as a result of the redevelopment of the Blackstone River

Valley. The reconfiguration of certain streets and intersections has taken place. It is hoped that the rehabilitation of several timeworn storefronts lining Greenwood Street and Blackstone River Road (formerly Millbury Street) will become a reality. Within the past twenty years, a new elementary school has been constructed, incorporating both a portion of the original school and the former Quinsigamond Library into its design; the former Quinsigamond Baptist Church has been moved and rehabilitated; and many of the decaying factory buildings of the former Southworks plant have been demolished and replaced with a Walmart. The vacant fire station is scheduled to undergo a renovation and be turned into offices for a local business. Earlier in 2015, ground was broken for the Blackstone Valley National Heritage Corridor Visitor's Center. A pamphlet designed by the Blackstone Valley National Heritage Corridor Commission portrays a Swedish millworker on its cover, promoting the Village as "Worcester's Little Sweden." In spite of these improvements, many storefronts remain in need of rehabilitation. Will the area see a rebirth? Many in the neighborhood remain skeptical but hopeful.

The gentrified Herbert Berg Florist building. Opened by Berg in the 1930s, the shop is now owned by Berg's longtime friend, Swedish-American Sally Jablonski. *Author's collection.*

In Quinsigamond Village, as in other former Swedish-American centers, landmarks remain as reminders of the past. In the Village, the original Swedish Evangelical Lutheran Emanuel Church building, several blocks from its modern counterpart, is now a community center, while the former IOGT Hall has been converted into artist studios. The former Quinsigamond Corps No. 2 Salvation Army building has been converted into a Hispanic church. Across the city on Belmont Street, three churches stand aside one another. In former days, they housed the Swedish-Finnish Lutheran Church, the First Swedish Baptist Church and the First Swedish Lutheran Church. Today, each edifice provides a sanctuary for different denominations, among them the Chinese Gospel Church. Indeed, numerous institutions, street names and churches remain as reminders of the once thriving structural community. An October 10, 2003 *Telegram and Gazette* article stated the fact succinctly: "Perhaps one of the most notable features of the city's Swedish community today is the ability to walk right by it and not notice it."

Chapter 6

SWEDISH-AMERICAN PUBLICATIONS IN WORCESTER

A brief mention should be made of the Swedish-language press in Worcester, as this area was of significance to community ties. The history of the Swedish-language press in America can be traced back to the 1850s. The first Scandinavian-language newspaper, *Skandinaven*, was published in New York in 1851 in Swedish and Dano-Norwegian. Four years later, the first purely Swedish-language newspaper, *Hemlandet, det Gamla och det Nya* (the *Homeland, the Old and the New*), was organized in Galesburg, Illinois. Eventually, the Swedish-American press became the second-largest ethnic press in the United States, behind German-American publications. Total estimates put the number of Swedish-American newspapers published at between six hundred and one thousand.

Worcester, as with all large Swedish-American centers in America, became home to a plethora of periodicals. Numerous Swedish-language publications, many of them short-lived, were printed prior to the turn of the century. In addition, numerous religious, humorous and social periodicals appeared and disappeared. Between 1883 and 1889, no fewer than seven had been published. In addition, no more than nine publications were started between 1894 and 1901. Some of the longest running included *Nya Fäderneslandet* (the *New Fatherland*, 1898–1901), *Skandinaviske Missionären* (the *Scandinavian Missionary*, 1902–7) and *Österns Weckoblad* (the *Eastern Weekly News*, 1896–1910?).

By 1900, such local and national Swedish-language publications were available at the A.P. Lundborg Bookstore on Main Street. Arriving in the

SKANDINAVIA
·GRUNDAD·
1886
Entered at the Post Office at Worcester, Mass., as second class mail matter.
Worcester, Mass., Onsdagen den 19 Mars 1913.

Skandinavia masthead. For its first year, it was published as *Worcester Veckoblad*. Within a decade of its 1885 founding, it was the largest Swedish-language newspaper east of Chicago. *Author's collection.*

city in 1889, Lundborg had, by the turn of the twentieth century, the largest Swedish bookstore east of Chicago.

The most successful of the Swedish-language weeklies were *Skandinavia* (1885–1918) and *Svea* (1897–1965). Each had correspondents in cities throughout New England. Both newspapers were key to the unity of the larger network of New England Swedes.

These newspapers eventually became part of larger publishing concerns, which catered to the business, organizational and religious needs of the community. The Swedish Publishing Company was parent to *Skandinavia*, while Svea Publishing Company published its namesake paper. In 1918, Svea Publishing acquired both *Skandinavia* and the *Swedish News* of Boston. This merger created a paper with a circulation of more than thirty thousand, making it the largest Swedish-American newspaper in the East and one of the largest in the United States. Wahlstrom estimated its circulation at around forty thousand in 1947. At its height, the paper consisted of twenty pages. By the time of Wahlstrom's thesis, it had been pared down to between twelve and sixteen pages.

The transition to English occurred in the post–World War II era, and by the end of the 1950s, English articles were interspersed throughout the paper. In December 1965, the Trulson family, owners of *Svea* since its inception, sold the concern to Swedish News Inc. of New York. *Svea* merged with *Nordstjernan* (the *North Star*) and was subsequently published under the *Nordstjernan-Svea* banner until 1992, when "Svea" was dropped from the name. Hence, the remaining legacy of the Swedish press in Worcester disappeared. It can be assumed that the purchase of *Svea* adversely affected the Worcester Swedish-American community, for it deprived the various organizational networks of their major source of advertising and broadcasting. At the time of its sale, *Svea* counted approximately twenty-six thousand subscribers both within and outside of the New England region.

SVEA

SWEDISH-AMERICAN NEWSPAPER

Advertisers find SVEA the best medium in order to reach the Swedish people in New England, where purchasing power is proverbial. Fully aware of its responsibility, SVEA has representatives in principal cities through-out the New England States. Main offices: 311 Main Street, Worcester 8, Massachusetts.

Nummer 49 — 57:de Årgången — Torsdagen den 3 December 1953

Starke Arvid *har fyllt sina modiga åttio år*

STOCKHOLM den 24 november. — Anders Arvid Andersson heter jag, noga räknat, men alla kallade mej för Starke Arvid på den tiden jag slog världsrekordet i tyngdlyftning. Nu sitter jag här bara och minns alltihop. Jo, nog är det riktigt att jag fylldes 80 år den 21 november.

— Vid nio års ålder låg jag sjuk i en konstig feber ett halvt år. Det var hemma i Värhulta vid Hjälmaren. Jag tyckte att jag såg eldkulor som for över huvudet på mej. Men när jag väl hade repat mej så vart jag starkare än någon annan. Det var som om allt ont hade rensats ur kroppen efter den där febern. Vid femton års ålder när jag gick och läste för prästen hjälpte jag till med tröskningen en dag. Då lyfte jag en tunna råg från golvet. Den stod i vägen. Jag tog tunnan först upp i knät, sen på logbalken och därefter upp på ryggen. Då visste jag att jag var stark, för den vägde åtskilligt över hundra kilo, bortåt hundratretti ungefär. Bondsäckarna som skulle till kvarn å malas var dryga förr.

Kungsholm har anlänt till New York

Sällskapsrum i turistklass, artistiskt inrett.

Svenska Amerika Liniens flaggskepp visas för allmänheten söndagen den 6 och måndagen den 7 december.

I dag, torsdagen den 3 december, har Svenska Amerika Liniens stolta flaggskepp den nya Kungsholm, anlänt till New York med 641 passagerare och därmed fullbordat sin jungfrufärd i västlig riktning. Som "julbåt" anträder Kungsholm återresan till Göteborg den 9 december.

Visning för turistlivet och pressen sker ombord på Kungsholm lördagen den 5 december. På söndagen den 6:te får allmänheten tillfälle att beskåda oceanpalatset vid visningar som pågår från 10 förmiddag till 8 på kvällen. Avgiften en dollar för äldre och 50 cent för barn går oavkortad som donation till välgörande ändamål i New York. Visningen på måndagskvällen mellan 5—8 är arrangerad av styrelsen för American-Scandinavian Foundation och Svenska Amerika Linien, varvid avgiften är $6.00 och inkomsten från visningen tillfaller stiftelsen. Vid detta tillfälle serveras förfriskningar och tenorsångaren Jussi Björling medverkar med en konsert.

Eugene O'Neill har avlidit i Boston

Amerikas främste dramatiker nobelpristagaren i litteratur år 1936, Eugene

Jordbrukare som lärare i folkskolor

En kurs av alldeles nytt slag för utbildning av lärare för

Many Swedish-American residents can still recall receiving *Svea*. For almost seventy years, the paper knitted the ethnic community together. The Worcester Public Library has *Svea* preserved on microfilm. *Author's collection.*

In addition to the ethnic press, the major Worcester newspapers catered to the Swedish-American community. Beginning in the 1920s and continuing into the early 1940s, the *Evening Gazette* carried the "News of the Swedish People" section where events were listed and noteworthy news items featured. The *Worcester Evening Post* also featured a Swedish news section and, on several occasions, published special supplements highlighting the achievements of the local Swedish-American community. These supplements were usually produced in conjunction with a special event or anniversary. To the best of the author's knowledge, no other ethnic group in Worcester was accorded this privilege. This preferential treatment illustrates the influential position that Swedish-Americans had obtained in Worcester.

Chapter 7

THE ORGANIZATIONAL NETWORK

A comprehensive review of the dozens of secular and religious groups that existed within the context of Swedish Worcester would itself fill a book. This chapter will take a look at a few of the groups that represented facets of what it meant to be Swedish in Worcester and how these groups were transformed over time. It should be noted, however, that the first fledgling organization, a musical quintet, was formed within the first year of Swedish settlement in Worcester. From there, a plethora of organizations for every need followed. These organizations helped to unite the ethnic community together and provided spiritual, financial and social needs that were of great importance to many. In relation to the various ethnic groups of Worcester, the Swedish-Americans developed the most extensive and diverse network of organizations centered on the ethnic community, including a private, nondenominational cemetery corporation and a hospital.

According to one source, the earliest secular organization formed by the Swedish immigrants was a male quintet, in 1869. For a time, this small group was associated with the local German-American organization *Gesang Verein Frohsinn*. Over the next few years, a Swedish literary group and a secondary musical group, the Swedish and Norwegian National Singing Club, were formed. These early Worcester societies are a prime example of ethnic cooperation among varying immigrant groups for survival purposes. As time progressed and some ethnic communities became stronger, these organizations faded.

"*Vi ska ställa till en roliger dans....*" Organized in 1941, the Swedish Folkdance Club entertained thousands during its thirty-year history. *Author's collection.*

The generational factor was a key ingredient in the maintenance of an ethnic identity. Wahlstrom noted in her thesis, for example, that the Thule Male Chorus, a local Swedish-American musical group, "perpetuates itself by the interest of father, son, and grandson. When one becomes too old, the other stands ready to take his place. Sometimes father and son sing side by side." This dependence on the generational maintenance would eventually detrimentally weaken the structural framework of the ethnic community. Karlson had already noted the process of amalgamation in 1910. However, he was astute enough to realize that assimilation also takes time, remarking that "the Swedish people have to be Swedish for quite a while yet." That the eventual assimilation of the community would occur was answered by Karlson's philosophy on the generational influences. "It is [first] the third generation that is really counted American," he stated. "By that time they have forgotten so much that they cannot be distinguished as foreigners." However, Karlson added his own reservations: "Whether this is a recommendable trait or not depends upon what point of view is taken."

The Scandinavian Women's Gymnastics Club (later the Scandinavian Women's Club) survived for more than eight decades, offering members camaraderie, support and good times, as illustrated in this November 1925 performance photograph. *Author's collection.*

Generational aspects aside, it was the goal of many Swedes to acclimate themselves to American culture as soon as possible. Thus, there is a multifaceted aspect to this identity creation—maintaining and inculcating Swedish traditions while at the same time adopting American customs and mannerisms within the framework of the Worcester experience. Hence, each facet of this identity seemed to augment the other. One could be a "good American" while at the same time maintaining traditional Swedish customs from the old country. It was a delicate balancing act that had consequences to it. For example, many elderly Swedish-Americans have told me with regret that they learned little Swedish from their parents, whose belief it was that in America one speak English. As early as 1910, Karlson remarked "There is hardly any people so plastic as the Swedish people…This is seen in the rapidity with which they assimilate new customs and traditions." Is there any doubt that the decline of "Swedishness" in Worcester was not a foregone

Impeccably dressed in their lodge regalia, officers of the Gustav V Lodge No. 118 of the Scandinavian Fraternity of America pose for a group portrait in the 1920s. This lodge was organized in Worcester in 1910. *Author's collection.*

conclusion based on the willingness of Swedes to promote themselves as good Americans?

The greater part of the secular Swedish-American organizations remained an indelible part of Worcester's cultural landscape for decades. They included the Scandinavian Women's Gymnastics Club, later reorganized into the benevolent Scandinavian Women's Club; the colorful and popular Swedish Folkdance Club; the Odin Club, made up of Swedish businessmen and professionals; the social clubs Svea Gille and Engelbrekt, both of which had quarters along the shores of Lake Quinsigamond; the Scandinavian Ski Club; and the Scandinavian Societies' Building Association (Lincoln Associates), which maintained a meetinghouse for member groups at 89 Lincoln Street until the construction of Interstate 290 doomed the historic building in the 1960s. The network of church-sponsored groups and local lodges of the various national Swedish organizations, such as the Vasa Order of America and the Scandinavian Fraternity of America, rounded out this dynamic structural community.

The very diversity of the community's religious institutions and the religious indifference of many in the community made any such all-encompassing religious organization unlikely. This set the Swedish-Americans apart from their ethnic counterparts. For example, the Franco-American community in Worcester was similar in size but did not have as varied or extensive a network of organizations. Several social and fraternal organizations did exist, but the majority of the societies were centered on the group's religious (Catholic) identity. Three Franco-American parishes (St. Joseph's, Notre-Dame-des-Canadiens and Holy Name of Jesus) were established, as was a Catholic orphanage, *Orphelinat Sainte-Anne* (St. Anne's Orphanage), organized in 1891. In 1885, the Notre-Dame-des-Canadiens parish cemetery was dedicated, and in 1903, *Le College de Assomption* (Assumption College), a Franco-American Catholic institution, was established in Greendale. Within the Polish community as well, community life centered on the parish church, Our Lady of Czestochowa, founded in 1902 and referred to as the "Soul of Polonia" in Worcester. The growth of the parish resulted in the organization of both a grammar school and a high school by 1936. Numerous civic and social organizations, such as the Polish National Alliance, celebrated both their ethnic and religious identity. For the area's Catholic groups, religion remained an indelible part of the ethnic identity of the respective community.

Some of the more notable organizations will now be looked at in the context of ethnic transformation. Of interest will be the affiliated lodges of the national organizations—most notably the International Order of Good Templars and the Vasa Order of America. The Swedish National Federation and its efforts in identity preservation will be studied, as will the more notable ethnic benevolent institutions such as the Swedish Cemetery Corporation and the Worcester Swedish Charitable Association. These organizations were chosen quite simply because information still exists. Unfortunately, much of the material dealing with many of the organizations that composed Swedish Worcester appears to have been lost to time. It is a great shame.

Identity and Morality: Swedish Temperance in Worcester

Founded in 1851 under the principles of "faith, hope, and charity," the International Organization of Good Templars (IOGT) was America's premier temperance movement; within the first twenty years, membership grew to more than 400,000. The Good Templars movement was transported to Sweden by Baptist preacher Olaf Bergström, who had witnessed the efforts of the organization during his stay in America. Upon returning to his native land, he organized the first lodge in Göteborg in 1879. The movement spread throughout Sweden, and within eight years, there were more than 1,500 lodges with a total membership of 60,000. The Good Templars crested in 1910 with 2,300 lodges and 160,000 members. For immigrating temperance-minded Swedes, to involve themselves in the temperance cause in the United States came naturally.

The IOGT established itself in Massachusetts in September 1858. In 1896, the Eastern Scandinavian Grand Lodge of IOGT of Massachusetts was established in order to capitalize on the growing numbers of Scandinavian-Americans who had immigrated to the Bay State, attracted by the state's numerous industrial centers. The organization of the first Swedish-speaking IOGT lodge in Massachusetts preceded the establishment of the District Lodge by five years. Residents of Quinsigamond Village, the city's premier Swedish district, formed Quinsigamonds Väl Lodge No. 1 of Worcester in 1891. In addition to Quinsigamonds Väl (Quinsigamond's Well-Being), the organized IOGT lodges that enjoyed long lifespans in Worcester were Kämpen (The Fighter, 1906) and Morgonstjärnan (Morning Star, 1911). In addition, several short-lived lodges were established; these included Eagle Lodge (1902–19) and Unity (1921–24). Two additional lodges, Ankaret (The Anchor) and Monitor were established in the 1890s but disbanded in 1901 and 1905, respectively.

Of the Worcester lodges, Quinsigamonds Väl and Kämpen were the most successful. A year after its founding, the former constructed a sizeable clubhouse on Ekman Street in the Village. At Indian Lake, Kämpen Lodge dedicated its summer quarters in 1929 on Sears Island, a unique campsite complete with electric lighthouse standing sentinel along the shore.

Industrial Worcester in the late nineteenth century was a potpourri of immigrant groups, with the Irish, French-Canadian and Swedish the most numerous. Competition for employment, social acceptance and social advancement could be fierce. As a result, the various ethnic communities were involved in a complex relationship: each group looked toward the Republican Protestant Yankee hierarchy for favor, but it also looked over its collective shoulders to see what its ethnic rivals were up to. A complex look at the politics of Swedish Worcester is outside this study, but it is worth noting and was covered in some depth by professors Estus and McClymer in *gå till Amerika.*

In this context, Swedish community leaders distanced themselves from their ethnic rivals, particularly the Irish, by highlighting their Protestant

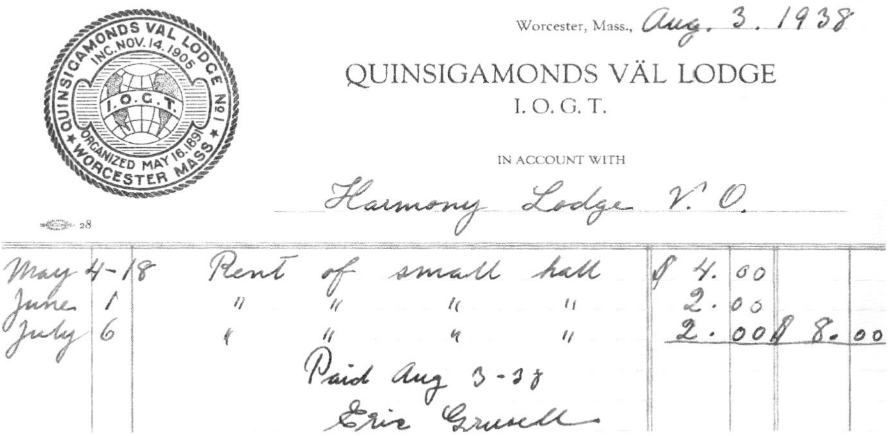

QUINSIGAMONDS VÄL LODGE No. 1 · INC. NOV. 14, 1905 · I. O. G. T. · ORGANIZED MAY 16, 1891 · WORCESTER MASS.

Worcester, Mass., Aug. 3. 1938

QUINSIGAMONDS VÄL LODGE

I. O. G. T.

IN ACCOUNT WITH

Harmony Lodge V. O.

May 4-18	Rent of small hall	$ 4.00		
June 1	" " " "	2.00		
July 6	" " " "	2.00	$ 8.00	

Paid Aug 3-38

Eric Grunell

Receipt for hall rental, 1938. The IOGT Hall owned by Quinsigamonds Väl Lodge No. 1 proved a popular meeting place for various Swedish groups within the Village neighborhood. *Author's collection.*

roots and supporting anti-alcohol campaigns, particularly during the city's annual vote in reference to the granting of liquor licenses. Author Timothy J. Meagher noted, "Indeed, when many Protestants abandoned the prohibitionist cause in the 1910s and 1920s, the Swedes emerged as the leaders and most zealous supporters of no-license."[66] The more conservative Swedish ministry and their congregants, mostly staunch evangelicals, supported the temperance cause, as did the IOGT. Local lodges even combined forces to support local candidates who stressed temperance. Even fellow Swedes were targeted. Swedish IOGT lodges banded together in 1899 to petition that no liquor license be granted to any city club, in an attempt to curtail drinking at Svea Gille, the city's premier Swedish organization. Even the few Swedish-owned saloons in operation came under pressure, for such establishments, it was felt, tarnished the good name that Scandinavians had made for themselves in Worcester.

Despite the activism, one should be cautious of placing too much emphasis on the influence of the Swedish IOGT. Karl Karlson noted in 1910 that the three Worcester IOGT lodges combined had a total membership of 286. In comparison with other local Swedish groups, these figures are quite small. For example, the John Ericsson Lodge No. 25, Vasa Order of America (fraternal), alone had a membership of 238 in 1910, or roughly 50 fewer persons than the combined membership of the IOGT lodges in Worcester.[67] Quinsigamonds Väl Lodge never recorded more than

200 members at any given time, while Kämpen Lodge had a membership of no more than 100 persons at any time during its existence. It has to be remembered, too, that not all the churches took such a rigid stance against alcohol, such as the Lutheran denominations.

Some even criticized the local IOGT lodges themselves. Reverend Karlson remarked that "each lodge is supposed to follow" a strict, temperance platform, but he complained that "the fact that they exist to a great extent through socials and aesthetics such as singing, music, elocution, etc. makes it difficult to do so." Indeed, local IOGT lodges sponsored literary circles, dance clubs and ethnic festivals, such as Midsummer. IOGT member Bror Joseph Rosenlund wrote about the 1917 festival, "*Framkomna till platsen, serverades Sill + Potatis samt Kaffee…Efter måltiden vidtog dans kring majstången.*" ("When we came out to the site, sill and potatoes together with coffee were served… After the meal, we all together danced around the maypole.")[68] In the 1890s, an IOGT summer camp was established along Lake Quinsigamond for the summer enjoyment of its members. For many, it was about temperance *and* being Swedish. However, all of this helped to solidify the public persona of *all* Swedes being largely temperate in nature.

Change was in the wind. By the 1930s, Kämpen Lodge No. 15, which had been organized as a young persons lodge, was willing to forego the Swedish language in order to maintain its youthful vigor. Interesting to note is the mindset of the younger set, many of whom were born in the United States and therefore more apt to accept and adjust to the question of language and identity. This younger set was comfortably *Swedish-American.*

However, the IOGT as a whole was on the wane by the immediate post–World War II era. In 1946, Kämpen Lodge was recognized as the largest in the Eastern Grand Lodge District, with eighty-five members. That same year, Engelbrekt Dahlström of Morgonstjärnan Lodge wrote, "In the middle twenties the membership began to dwindle…The few of us who still hold on to our charter believe that other days are coming, a new era, a new world." Noted, too, was the general decline in membership throughout the nation, which had caused whole districts to fold. By 1946, there were only thirteen lodges remaining within Massachusetts, despite the fact that sixty-nine lodges had been established since 1891.

As with other local Swedish-American organizations, the very makeup of the IOGT lodges was transformed as the Swedish language and purely Scandinavian affiliation were replaced by a more mainstream identity. In 1935, the Swedish language within the Massachusetts District was officially dropped in favor of English. The change was cosmetic, as English had been

Kämpen Lodge No. 15 members pose for the photographer at a group outing, circa 1920. Such outings strengthened the bonds of brotherhood. *Author's collection.*

in use for the better part of a decade at both public and private meetings. Some lodges, however, retained the Swedish language. In fact, of the thirteen active lodges that submitted histories to the fiftieth-anniversary book in 1946, three were written in Swedish.

Four years after English had been officially adopted, the district voted to change its name in an attempt to broaden its appeal. Hence, the Eastern Scandinavian Grand Lodge of IOGT of Massachusetts became the Eastern Grand Lodge of the IOGT in 1939. In connection with this change came the following lamentation on the loss of Swedish:

> *Changing the language is not as easy as some people think. It is far more than just a few new words to learn in order to get by. A language carries with it a new way of thinking...Literature and rituals are translated but no matter how masterfully it is done, it will never be the same as the original. The familiar phrases so well remembered when learned in the mother tongue become flat and strange in another language, no matter how well you understand it. The impression in your mind will never be the same.*[69]

This statement reflects on the importance of the Swedish language to the sense of individual identity, particularly for those first-generation Swedish-born immigrants. Many ethnic pundits throughout the country predicted that the loss of language signified the end of the Swedish-American identity, and various debates on this topic raged throughout the ethnic community in the early part of the twentieth century. Although this was not necessarily the case, the replacement of the Swedish language within an organization such as the IOGT represented a loss in personal identity. The IOGT suffered from American cultural shifts as well. In the quickening pace of postwar American society, the IOGT and its counterparts fell victim to "the changing mores adopted by the new, urban professional middle class, mores that included social drinking. Temperance advocates both within and without the ethnic community were increasingly perceived as old-fashioned and parochial."[70] The IOGT was fighting a losing battle in the face of overwhelming social and cultural shifts. Despite this, many adherents held firm in their convictions. Having lost a family member to alcoholism in 1947, IOGT member Bror Joseph "Joe" Rosenlund wrote bitterly that "his early death can be blamed on the liquor, may those bartenders and saloon-keepers who so gladly took his money suffer for their actions."[71]

In 1967, Quinsigamonds Väl Lodge sold its Ekman Street headquarters to Quinsigamond Lodge No. 517 of the Vasa Order, which rededicated the building as Vasa Hall. Today, it is home to the Worcester County Poetry Association. Kämpen Lodge continued to meet at its summer clubhouse on Sears Island until the 1980s, when it finally sold its property as well. The clubhouse has since been converted into a private residence; the lighthouse survives as a reminder of what once was and can been viewed while driving on Grove Street along Indian Lake.

Although the group dynamic of the Good Templars faded from view, members persevered in a personal and private manner. "We had our Good Templar meeting yesterday at our home," wrote Kämpen Lodge member Alice Carlson in 1983. "We are just family, about 15 in all; the Good Templars in our area are just about gone, but we will still practice what we preach, so it looks like we will be Good Templars the rest of our lives." As with many surviving members of the IOGT, she and her husband, Sven, held true to their convictions until their passing.[72]

Identity and Brotherhood: The Vasa Order in Worcester

The Vasa Order of America is today the largest of the remaining Swedish-American fraternal organizations. Organized in Connecticut in 1896, it was born during the period of flourishing Swedish-American institutions. Numerous national organizations were inaugurated, including the Independent Order of Vikings, Ancient Order of Svithiod,

Scandinavian Fraternity of America and the American Union of Swedish Singers.

The Order takes its name from King Gustav Vasa, the founder of modern Sweden. The organizational makeup of the Vasa Order is as follows: a national Grand Lodge oversees District Lodges, which are broken down geographically. Within each District Lodge exist the various local lodges. The Order is currently composed of no more than three hundred local lodges throughout America, Canada and Sweden. The Vasa motto is "*Sanning och Enighet*," or "Truth and Unity."

Both the Order and Massachusetts District No. 2 reached their peak in 1929. National membership stood at 72,261 members, with slightly over 15,000, or one-fifth of the Order's membership, under the jurisdiction of the Massachusetts District Lodge. Between 1907 and 1958, Massachusetts was the largest district in the Order in terms of membership. However, there has been steady erosion in membership since 1929. Between 1929 and 1970, the Order lost half of its members. In 2001, the national membership registered no more than 19,200 members. The Massachusetts district mirrored this precipitous decline, falling under 10,000 members by 1950 and fewer than 5,000 by 1966. The Massachusetts District currently faces a membership crisis, as enrollments have fallen sharply within the last decade. As of 2015, membership hovers around 600 members in eight local lodges. At the current rate of decline, Philip Becker, Massachusetts District No. 2 Historian, has estimated the demise of the Order by 2030. It should be noted that at least two of the District Lodges have maintained an active and steady membership (both in Sweden), but the overall trend outweighs these small gains. It would be ironic if the Order—established in America—were to one day survive only in Sweden.

In Massachusetts, the first lodge of the Order, Ragnar No. 10, was incorporated in Worcester a year before the establishment of the District Lodge in 1899. By 1903, there were three additional lodges in the city: Flora No. 15 (for Swedish-American women), John Ericsson No. 25 and Victoria No. 43 (for Swedish-American women). The greatest growth in Worcester occurred during the 1920s, when seven lodges were established between 1920 and 1929. Additionally, Charles Lindbergh Lodge No. 520 was incorporated in Auburn in 1928 and transferred to Worcester around 1960. In 1922, the Vasa Committee, a unifying body composed of representatives from the Worcester lodges, was formed to coordinate affairs and promote the Order. Worcester has always been the most influential city in the district. For example, in 1942, the total district membership was 11,598, with the

The John Ericsson Lodge No. 25 chorus, 1920. Organized in 1900, the lodge took its name from the designer of the Civil War ironclad *Monitor*. *Author's collection.*

Worcester lodges representing 3,495 of the total, or roughly 30 percent. In 1974, the district membership had dropped to 3,050, with 937 members of the Worcester lodges. Again the percentage of district membership stood at roughly 30 percent. It should also be noted that at one point, the John Ericsson Lodge No. 25 in Worcester was the largest lodge in the Order, with more than 800 members at its peak.

The decline in the Swedish language among the Worcester lodges took place over an extended period of time. Consequently, it was these fraternal secular lodges, not the churches, that preserved the language in the Worcester area well into the second half of the twentieth century. Wahlstrom, in her 1947 thesis, noted that within Vasa, "Swedish is the official language… It should be further noted that only four of the lodges use English as the official language. Swedish is predominantly used." Her experiences with the Worcester-area Vasa lodges contrasted sharply the state of the Swedish-organized churches at the time, where Swedish had largely disappeared from religious services. Maintenance of the Swedish language, although an important cultural facet for older members, may also be viewed as a barrier in the recruitment of younger Swedish-Americans, many of whom did not possess a mastery, or even rudimentary knowledge, of the language. The institution of Nordic Lodge No. 611 in Worcester is illustrative of an attempt to encourage non-Swedish speakers—aka young Swedish-Americans—to join, as this lodge was the first in the city to be organized strictly as an English-speaking lodge in 1939.

Records of the Massachusetts District No. 2 Annual Convention were kept in Swedish until 1948, at which time they were printed in English. A survey of the Worcester lodges over the course of the next decade shows a progression toward the use of English as well. For example, within a decade after Wahlstrom's observation that four of ten Worcester lodges were using English, by 1958 five of the eight remaining lodges were English-speaking. As late as 1967, the John Ericsson Lodge No. 25, remained the last Swedish-speaking lodge in Worcester. In 1953, this lodge did request information from the district concerning bilingual meetings. In reply, District Secretary Einor Holm replied that it was up to the discretion of the lodge to "use a language…understood of all your members present." He warily added, "Bear in mind that by obliterating the Swedish language and customs, or let us call it 'americanizing' [*sic*] your lodge, you have taken away something from your old Swedish born members you will be unable to replace. The decision is up to your members." Holm then cautioned the lodge "from hastily doing something you may later regret."[73]

The loss of Swedish within the Worcester lodges was not unique. Existing district correspondence between 1948 and 1955 noted that several lodges petitioned for a language change. Coinciding with this development, a few lodges also petitioned for a change in their bylaws, requesting the omission of "Swedish extraction" in favor of "Scandinavian extraction" as a requirement for membership. Thus the switch to English and the broadening of membership requirements can be seen as an effort to increase the flagging memberships within the various District Lodges. Today, ancestral requirements have ceased. According to the Order's website, membership is now open to non-Nordic persons "committed to the promotion and advancement of Swedish and Nordic heritage and culture."

The Swedish language was an important part of the identity of this fraternal organization, as it had been for the churches and other Swedish-American organizations in the community. The 1946 fifty-year Vasa Order history, in fact, is written completely in the Swedish language, unlike the IOGT history published the same year and quoted previously. In 1946, Grand Lodge Cultural Leader Bror Munson noted the decline in membership and realized that the Order could no longer count on the younger generation maintaining the lodge memberships. Times had changed, Munson realized, and new methods must be developed (translation by author):

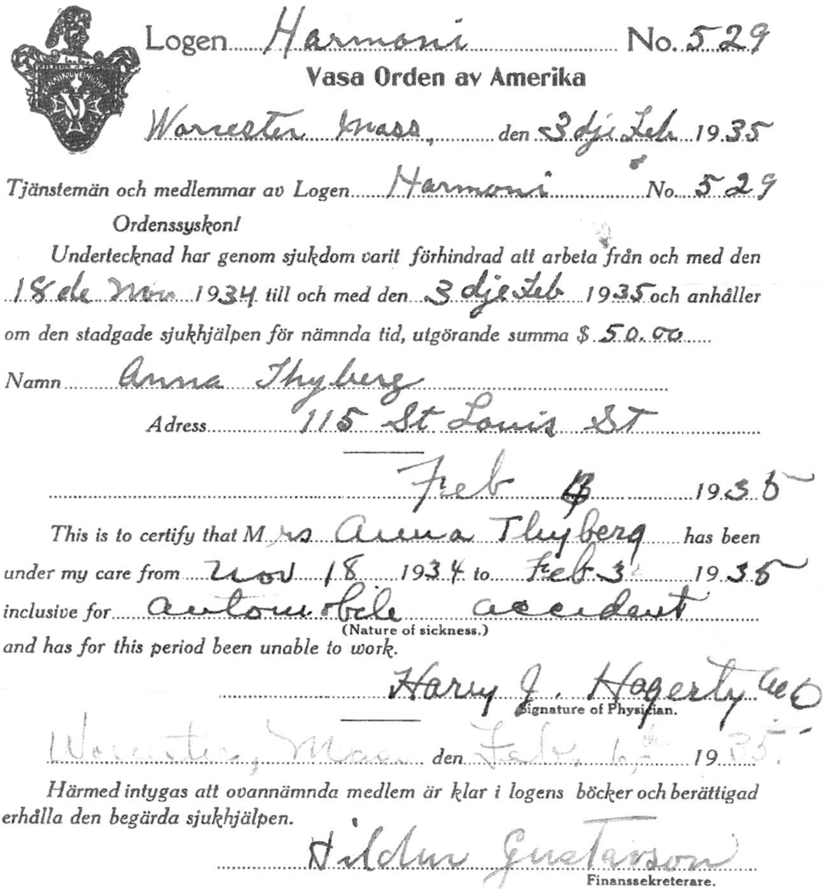

Logen Harmoni No. 529

Vasa Orden av Amerika

Worcester Mass., den 3dje Feb 1935

Tjänstemän och medlemmar av Logen Harmoni *No.* 529

Ordenssyskon!

Undertecknad har genom sjukdom varit förhindrad att arbeta från och med den 18de Nov 1934 *till och med den* 3dje Feb 1935 *och anhåller om den stadgade sjukhjälpen för nämnda tid, utgörande summa $* 50.00

Namn Anna Thyberg

Adress 115 St Louis St

Feb 4 1935

*This is to certify that M*rs Anna Thyberg *has been under my care from* Nov 18 1934 *to* Feb 3 1935 *inclusive for* automobile accident
(Nature of sickness.)
and has for this period been unable to work.

Harry J. Hagerty MD
Signature of Physician.

Worcester, Mass. *den* Feb. 6th 1935

Härmed intygas att ovannämnda medlem är klar i logens böcker och berättigad erhålla den begärda sjukhjälpen.

Hildur Gustavson
Finanssekreterare.

The Vasa Order provided its members with a host of benefits. In 1935, member Anna Thyberg received fifty dollars toward medical expenses after an automobile accident. Note the use of dual languages on the form. *Author's collection.*

> *Ungdomarna i våra logar äro icke födda i Sverige. De inga inte i logerna av samma anledning som ungdomarna för femtio år sedan. Dessa sökte vänskap och umgänge, och in många fall ingicks giftermål mellan medlemmar av samma loge, vilket var en bidragande orsak att kvarstå i logen. Nu däremot, om en medlem gifter sig kan det vara med en person, som inte tillhör logen, som kanske är av en annan stam, vilket i många fall gör att medlemmen utgår ur logen.*
>
> *Därför måste andra dragningskrafter uppfinnas och ut nyttjas för att kvarhålla den yngre generationen i våra loger, varvid det naturligtvis är viktigt att verka för bibehållandet av vårt svenska språk.*[74]

> [The youth in our lodges were not born in Sweden. They do not enter the lodges for the same reasons as the youth of fifty years ago. They searched for friendship and company, and in many cases members of the same lodge entered into marriage, which was a contributing cause in remaining with the lodge. Now on the other hand, if a member marries it may be to one who does not belong to the lodge, who might be of another heritage, which in many cases results in the member withdrawing from the lodge.
>
> Therefore other attractions must be devised and made use of to detain the younger generation in our lodges, which as a matter of course is of importance for the preservation of our Swedish language.]

Munson correctly assumed that the generational differences had to be handled with new and improved methods of recruitment, but he failed to see the greatest barrier: the Swedish language. The second and third American-born generations were largely ignorant of Swedish. It was therefore asking the impossible to seek the retention of younger members in an organization whose language they did not speak. Efforts within the Order to address language met with limited success, and by the 1960s, the Vasa Order had become a largely English-speaking organization, while membership continued its decline. The Worcester lodges mirrored this trend.

The Vasa Order had made great efforts in the preservation of the Swedish culture in America. Celebrated trips to Sweden were organized for the Order's fledgling youth groups in 1924, 1929 and 1933 and subsequently published as *Vasabarnens från Amerika: Trenne Resor i Far och Mors Land* (*The Vasa Children from America: Three Trips to Father and Mother's Country*). Additional tours were undertaken in 1963 and 1973. Popular "Vasa Flights" sponsored by Massachusetts District No. 2 were chartered to Sweden during the 1960s; the noted Rosenlund Travel Agency in Worcester handled the details. In Worcester, Vasa lodges sponsored youth groups during the 1930s, the most popular being the Framåt (Forward) Club, whose members participated in local Swedish-American events. Unfortunately, most all youth groups within the district have folded.

The decline of the Order in Worcester took place in two stages. In the 1950s, a good many lodges were merged in an attempt to maintain solvency. Between 1950 and 1960, four mergers took place. Another series of mergers and dissolutions occurred between 1984 and 1992 that resulted in three surviving lodges in Worcester. It is unfortunate that these three remaining

Alice Carlson from Millbury became the first female Grand Master of the Vasa Order in 1982 and in 1987 was voted Swedish-American of the Year. She and husband Sven were Vasa members for more than sixty years. *Author's collection.*

lodges did not pool their resources and act collectively as a cohesive group working toward a common goal: the preservation of a Swedish legacy in the Worcester area. Rather, each remained a separate entity, with little cooperation between them. Based on personal experience, it is my opinion that at times the Worcester Swedes can be their own worst enemies, allowing personal jealousies and rivalries of years past to stand in the way of common objectives. By 2012, only one Vasa lodge remained: Nordic No. 611. This particular lodge continues to function as an active organization with a membership hovering around two hundred. In the western part of the state, Viking Lodge No. 756 was organized in Greenfield as late as 2000.

The change in attitudes reflected a change in ethnic identity. Second- and third-generation Swedish-Americans were no exception. Swedish-American youth during this period may have participated in ethnic events; indeed, some may have involved themselves in the ethnic community. Their involvement, however, was based on different experiences. These members had been born and raised within an American framework, and as such, there was no personal tie to Sweden. "*Far och Mors land*" (Father and Mother's land), as well as the Swedish language, became a *symbol* of what it meant to be Swedish-American. There was no personal connection to either language or birthplace; rather, these two facets became one of a host of identifying traits within the context of a Swedish-American identity, and these traits were more personal in nature. Thus, learning a few phrases or words seems "Swedish" enough for some, while for others the language remains unintelligible. A few may even take a Swedish language course and learn to speak rudimentary Swedish, but this is the exception. Historian H. Arnold Barton has stated that the Swedish language today is heard for purely "sentimental reasons before a largely uncomprehending public." The Swedish-American experience in Worcester has mirrored this transformation of ethnicity.

Ethnic Maintenance: The Swedish National Federation

The Swedish National Federation (SNF) was organized in 1911 out of the disbandment of the former *Svenska-Amerikanska Förbundet* (Swedish-American Federation). Its very founding reflected the need for a central organizational body that could bring together the various Swedish-American establishments within Worcester. The federation is composed of member groups, who are represented at meetings by delegates. The number of delegates was originally based on an organization's membership, although this requirement has since been abandoned. The purpose of the SNF was, and is, to "preserve and develop the social and cultural heritage that Sweden has bequeathed America; to represent the interests of the folk whose ancestry is Swedish."[75]

The blending of this dual Swedish and American identity is prevalent in the seal of the federation. Designed in 1916 by delegates Reuben Heidenblad, Axel Rosenlund and Emil Rolander, the seal was officially adopted in March

The seal of the Swedish National Federation highlights the dual Swedish and American identity of its founders. *Author's collection.*

of that year. It depicts mothers Columbia and Svea, each holding her respective shield and pointing to her country on the globe. The flags of each country fly in the background. It was introduced publicly at the 1916 Midsummer Festival. Noted the *Worcester Evening Gazette* on March 4, 1916, "The coat-of-arms as a whole is scheduled to make a notable impression with the Swedish residents of Worcester."

The SNF quickly became the premier organization in Worcester. Originally represented by ten organizations, membership in the federation grew to nineteen organizations with 102 delegates within a decade. On February 3, 1941, federation secretary John Sands reported, "The makeup of the Federation 1940 were as follows; there was 102 delegates…representing 34 different organizations, which in turn representing nearly 10,000 Swedish-American peoples." By 1948, the membership had expanded to thirty-six groups and 129 delegates. Membership in the federation seems to have peaked in the 1950s and then entered into a decline as the various member groups either merged with other organizations or disbanded. The loss of membership hastened in the 1970s, when many longtime organizations disbanded. Currently, the federation is composed of a few member groups with fewer than 20 delegates. Thus, as the representative organization of Swedish Worcester, the decline of the federation mirrors the decline of the structural community overall.

Unfortunately, no records can be found indicating when English became the standard language of the SNF. It can best be estimated that the change occurred sometime between 1927 and 1938, which would place the federation within the timeframe when the language issue was being discussed within numerous Swedish-American congregations and organizations. The concerns relating to language and ethnic identity compelled the federation in 1936 to petition the Worcester School Committee for a three-year course in Swedish. The development of a Swedish course for the Worcester schools was seen as a way of perpetuating the familial (i.e., communal) ties:

> *The practical value of Swedish particularly for children of Swedish parents, we believe, will also be readily admitted by most people who will not fail to realize that a closer contact will be established between the parents and the schools as well as between the parents and the children...With the large number of the Swedish parents in Worcester it has for many years been one hope and desire that their children should be given the same opportunity to learn the language of their fathers as have children of French, German or Spanish parentage.*[76]

The petition could also be viewed as an attempt to place Swedish on an even par with the so-called traditional school language courses such as those listed earlier. In any event, the school committee approved this request, and for several years, Swedish was taught in the city's high schools. This can be seen as a significant fact; the 1943 *American Swedish Handbook* lists only eight high school Swedish courses nationwide. Five of these were located in Minnesota, with the remaining in Illinois; Jamestown, New York; and Worcester. The establishment of such a course, however, does not seem to have helped in the perpetuation of the Swedish language in Worcester.

The federation was instrumental in the building of the ethnic community. In 1915, the Skandia Bank and Trust Company was

Reflecting its Scandinavian roots, the Viking ship logo of Guarantee Bank is well remembered by generations of area residents. *Author's collection.*

established with assistance from the federation to provide low-cost house mortgages to the Scandinavian-American community. This credit union grew to become the largest of its kind in the United States by 1930, when it was granted a banking charter by the state. At that time, assets were in excess of $1,400,000. Four years later, the establishment was renamed Guarantee Bank and Trust; the renamed institution even sported a new Viking Ship logo. Well into the 1960s, the majority of bank directors were of Swedish descent. The bank's new owners phased out the Viking Ship logo in 1977, while Guarantee Bank was eventually swallowed up during the period of the great bank mergers in the 1980s. Its success as both an ethnic and financial institution can be gauged by the great support given its initial incorporation and the lifespan the institution enjoyed within the larger Worcester community.

In addition to Guarantee Bank, the establishment of Fairlawn Hospital was perhaps the greatest achievement of the SNF. The committee selected to study the issue in early 1921 made the desire for such an ethnic institution clear (translation by author):

> *Vi anse att förefinnas behof af ett sjukhus med uppgift att vårda de sjuka landsmän och landsmanninor i Worcester och New England. Det är ofta endast med svårighet de våra kunda förmås söka lasarettvård när sådan erfodras, emedan de känna sig som främlingar bland främlingar och understundom oförmågna att förstå andra eller göra sig själfva förstådda.*[77]
>
> [We think that there exists a need of a hospital with a mission to take care of the sick countrymen and countrywomen in Worcester and New England. It is often only with difficulty our people are able to search for hospital care when such is required, because they feel themselves strangers among foreigners and at times incapable of understanding another or making themselves understood.]

At the same time representatives were discussing the formation of a hospital for their fellow countrymen, the Fairlawn estate came up for sale. Constructed in 1893, the estate was well known by local inhabitants as the residence of James A. Norcross, one of the area's premier builders, whose work was recognized both locally and nationally. Fronting May Street, the spacious estate spanned several acres between Lovell and June Streets and included a small pond and frontage along the shores of Coes Pond. Following private negotiations, an option was secured, and it was reported at a subcommittee meeting that the property could be purchased for $60,000 (about $725,000 in 2015). A mass meeting was held on June 6, 1921, and thirty-eight Swedish businessmen pledged $33,000 toward the purchase price. The Scandinavian-American community was then canvassed, which brought in an additional $100,000 in pledges, a significant sum for the time.

Following renovations, Fairlawn Hospital opened the following year. The establishment of the hospital was cause for celebration within the ethnic community; *Svea* had labeled the hospital "*En Svensk Monument*" ("A Swedish Monument"). Henceforth, the federation maintained a lifelong affiliation with Fairlawn, donating monies for the purchase of equipment and

PLEDGE $10,000 FOR HOSPITAL

Swedish Business Men at Meeting Promise Aid to Fairlawn

OCT 2 1 1925

Ten thousant dollars was pledged as a guaranty fund against a possible deficit in the running expenses of the Fairlawn hospital at the end of this year, at a meeting and supper last night in New Bay State Hotel by about 100 leading Swedish business and professional men of this city.

Nils Bjork, president of the hospital board, presided. Ex-Mayor Pehr G. Holmes, vice president; Victor E. Runo, legal adviser, and Dr. F. Julius Quist, former president of the medical staff, were the speakers.

The successful work of the hospital so far was reviewed, and the future needs of the institution were outlined. A round-table conference followed the addresses.

The Swedish-American community supported Fairlawn Hospital financially in its early years in order to ensure the institution's survival. *Author's collection.*

establishing a free bed fund for the Swedish-American community's needy residents. This association ended following the conversion of the hospital into a rehabilitation facility in 1987. Unfortunately for the researcher, all records pertaining to the original institution were destroyed during the conversion process.

Fairlawn Hospital epitomized Swedish-American benevolence. Its effects stretched far beyond the ethnic community, as the hospital very quickly became noted for its quality of care. The *Worcester Evening Post* remarked in a November 1, 1928 article that "we may feel justly proud of our Scandinavian citizenship, in the cause of ministering unto the sick, regardless of race or creed." The success of the hospital as a mainstream institution can be seen

Swedish National Federation president Frances Gadde honors Alice Carlson as Swedish-American Woman of the Year at the 1972 Midsummer Festival at SAC Park. *Author's collection.*

in a computation of patients served between 1936 and 1941. Of those numbers, 53 percent were American-born, 21 percent were Scandinavian-born and 26 percent were of "other origins."[78] Conceived as an ethnic institution, Fairlawn Hospital rapidly became a mainstream facility, serving the community at large. Despite this, throughout the majority of its lifespan as a general medical facility, the area community commonly referred to Fairlawn as "the Swedish hospital." The 1987 sale and conversion closed another chapter of the Swedish-American story in Worcester.

The greatest display of Swedish-American ethnicity was the federation's annual Midsummer Festival. The first festival and parade in 1912 was an exceptional event. More than 4,000 participants representing dozens of organizations entertained a crowd of 100,000 spectators. The July 1912 issue of *Worcester Magazine* stated that the Midsummer Festival "was without doubt the greatest celebration ever conducted by people of a single foreign nativity living within the boundaries of this city." Indeed, the Swedish weekly *Skandinavia* chimed in to say that such displays of ethnic pride constituted "the idea of the Swedish nationality." These early ethnic spectacles were also intended to highlight the favored status that the Swedes had achieved for themselves in the Worcester area. Midsummer, the great holiday born out of the Romantic period, continues to be sponsored by the SNF and throughout the years has played host to notable American and Swedish personalities, among them Congressman Christian Herter

Dr. Edwin T. Olson is seen filming the Swedish Folkdance Club performance at a 1940s Midsummer Festival at SAC Park. *Author's collection.*

and Swedish ambassador Gunnar Jarring. In 1926, during their tour of America, Crown Prince Gustaf Adolf and Princess Louise were honored guests. Beginning in 1941 and continuing for five years, the federation began the practice of filming the festival in color. Copies of these vintage celebrations exist today.

Perhaps the most recognizable personality of the Midsummer celebration was accordionist Nils Lundin. Beginning in the 1950s, Lundin's performances at the summer event were a welcome staple for more than fifty years. Although based at Braintree's Viking Club outside Boston, Lundin was well known in the Greater Worcester area as the star performer on the *SAC Party* radio show, hosted by the effervescent Paul Larson. Beginning in 1955 and running into the 1970s, this dance program was broadcast live every Saturday night from the Dome Room at SAC Park over station WORC in Worcester. In 1980, the Massachusetts House of Representatives named Lundin "Man of the Year." A virtuoso, Lundin's musical abilities were also recognized by Sweden. In 1981, he was presented with a medal from the king for his efforts in preserving Swedish musical traditions, and his "Wooden Shoe Polka" won him the prestigious Elin Award, the Swedish equivalent of a Grammy. Lundin's passing in December 2014 at the age of ninety-three brought to a close a remarkable musical career that spanned over seven decades.

Larson himself was a favorite of the Swedish-American community and would go on to host another program. The *Scandinavian Hour* was a Sunday morning staple for years on station WNEB and, later, WORC. I have vivid memories of Sunday breakfast with my family listening to Larson pontificate about the merits of pastry from Helen's Bakery before announcing another accordion favorite.

Midsummer is the last public celebration of a Swedish-American identity in the Worcester area. Former federation-sponsored events, such as the annual Lucia (Christmas) Ball, were discontinued in the 1980s. Beginning in 2003, as a way in which to recognize the efforts of those involved in identity preservation, the SNF began awarding an annual Heritage Award. The following individuals have been recipients: Bob and Norma Belden (2003), Leif and Siw Kristiansson (2004), Eunice Nelson (2005), Susan Johnson (2006), Eric J. Salomonsson (2007), Elaine Barrows (2008), Robin Forsberg (2009), William O. Hultgren (2010), Philip C. Becker (2011) and Larry Stidsen (2012).

Through its efforts, the Swedish National Federation provided the overall ethnic community with a unifying governing body, which in turn, afforded the

Federation members gather at the 1999 scholarship awards. *Sitting, left to right*: Eric J. Salomonsson, Marge Stake and Carl Johansson. *Standing, left to right*: Norma Belden, Rose Erikson, Alice and Sven Carlson, Eunice Nelson, Susan T. Johnson and Bob Belden. *Author's collection.*

federation an ample amount of resources from within the ethnic community. These resources allowed the federation to construct and maintain not only a local ethnic identity but also "monuments" (i.e., physical structures) to the community.

The federation's greatest period of influence began with its 1911 founding and continued well into the 1960s. Afterward, the organization lost much of its member base due to the increasing loss of the various organizations within Swedish Worcester. Although the member base has held over the past several years, the lack of new delegates and the advanced average age of the current roster pose a threat from within.

For many of these reasons, the federation felt it imperative to secure the future of its scholarship program, a staple since 1919. In January 2002, the federation co-sponsored the establishment of a $75,000 scholarship fund for high school students of Scandinavian descent. (This included the Arnold and Sylvia Nylund Fund.) Now managed by the Greater Worcester Community Foundation, the scholarship program, as well as the federation namesake, will continue to survive should the disbandment of the organization occur. As with The Lutheran Home and Fairlawn, this scholarship fund will be a continuing legacy of Swedish-American benevolence in the Worcester area.

Identity and Eternal Rest: The Swedish Cemetery Corporation

The transition from a purely ethnic corporation to a mainstream American establishment is best reflected in the history of the Swedish Cemetery Corporation. The very establishment of the corporation is unique, for this concern is the only known nondenominational private cemetery corporation begun by Swedish immigrants in the United States. Swedish sections of public cemeteries and individual church graveyards do exist, but no corporation devoted to the internment of Swedish-Americans is known with the exception of Worcester. This very fact is proof of the extensive and unique organizational framework that existed within the Worcester ethnic community.

"We have long felt the need, as a nation, of having a cemetery that we could call our own. But partly, because the wages of the people were small and partly that the Americans have been kind enough to let us bury our dead in a small slip of their cemetery (Hope), we did not do anything about it." So wrote the famous Methodist pastor and cemetery advocate Daniel Sörlin in his diary in 1885. In the summer of that year, land was purchased on Webster Street and organizational meetings held that autumn. On Memorial Day 1886, the Swedish Cemetery was officially dedicated. On June 1, a reporter from the *Worcester Telegram* wrote, "These people have come to stay. They have established their co-operative stores, organized their religious societies and erected their houses of worship, while yesterday witnesseth the dedication of their cemetery." The 1886 dedication marked the beginning of the Memorial Day service tradition that continues to date.

The popularity of the cemetery within the ethnic community resulted in the expansion of the original burial ground and the subsequent establishment of a second site, located within a mile of the original resting place. This second location, purchased in the spring of 1921, satisfied the needs of the community for generations. The two sites were officially designated Old Swedish Cemetery and New Swedish Cemetery in 1924.

In its first half century, the corporation supported the ethnic community by providing employment to those who needed financial assistance and by

Left: Flanked by the Swedish and American flags, the memorial marker at the entrance to Old Swedish Cemetery pays homage to its founders. *Author's collection.*

Below: This 1961 aerial view of New Swedish Cemetery (now All Faiths) shows its bucolic location surrounded by Leesville Pond in Worcester. *Author's collection.*

funding the burials of those who could not afford such services. For several years, free burials made up over half of those interred. The 1896 report, for example, listed a total of 1,032 burials, with 642 having been placed within the corporation's free section. In addition, a plot of land was laid out in 1929 for burials from the Swedish Lutheran Old People's Home, which had been established on Harvard Street at the beginning of the decade.

The transition of the corporation from a purely Swedish ethnic institution began during the 1930s. By 1934, the superintendent's and treasurer's reports were largely recorded in the English language. The minutes of the director's meetings were kept in Swedish until September 1941, when illness forced longtime secretary Emil T. Rolander into retirement. That same year, the Memorial Day program was printed in English for the first time.

The corporation's Memorial Day services were transformed as well. In 1929, the corporation decided to celebrate concurrent exercises at both cemeteries, a practice that continued until 1945. Prior to 1936, both services were entirely in Swedish. On Memorial Day that year, the corporation celebrated the fiftieth anniversary of the dedication of its first cemetery. A memorial marker honoring the founders was placed at the entrance of the old cemetery, and a history of the corporation was issued in English. The celebration also marked the introduction of English into the Memorial Day program. Six years later, on May 8, 1942, the board of directors voted that both Memorial Day programs were "to be all English." On May 11, 1945, the language question was permanently settled when the board of directors concluded "all speaking at the Memorial services be in English except that the Minister that is chosen to speak may introduce some Swedish on his own initiative."

Throughout the majority of the 1950s, Swedish hymns were included in the Memorial Day services, but their use seems to have largely disappeared by the early 1960s. The loss of Swedish in the Memorial Day services was brought to the corporation's attention in 1965, when the Swedish National Federation noted in a letter that "something has been missing in the Memorial Day exercises…This something is a vital part of our National heritage—the Swedish language, our mother tongue, which should be kept alive." In reply, Secretary Sigurd B. Falling expressed the corporation's understanding of the "vital part" that language played in national heritage but also expressed the reality of the situation, noting that "at the present time there is only one minister in the local area capable of speaking Swedish fluently and many of the churches of Swedish background no longer have ministers who are of Swedish descent."[79] This reply is interesting for it noted the continued transformations occurring within the area's Swedish-American congregations—transformations previously observed by Wahlstrom in her 1947 thesis.

Language was only one facet in the transition of the corporation from a purely ethnic to more mainstream institution. A seventy-five-year history noted in 1961:

> *There was a time when the privilege of buying lots in the Cemetery was limited to people of Swedish descent but now there is no nationality restriction of any kind. Directors have sometimes even sadly pondered the possibility of omitting the word "Swedish" from the name of the Cemetery. In the present By-laws…there is no reference to "Swedish," except on the cover…There will doubtless be a time when awareness of the Swedish heritage will come only with outside reminder.*[80]

The possibility of renaming the corporation was brought up at a February 1959 director's meeting but was tabled without further discussion. By the early 1970s, however, talks began in earnest. Between 1973 and 1976, discussions were held on the subject, and several names were suggested, among them Fairlawn, Woodland Park, Memory Lane, Oakwood, Island View and Upsala Memorial. In 1974, the name Evergreen Memorial Cemetery was agreed on but was dropped due to foreseen conflicts with Evergreen Cemetery in neighboring Leominster, Massachusetts. By the end of 1975, the directors had agreed on Faith Cemetery Corporation Inc.; Old and New Swedish cemeteries were renamed Faith Cemetery North and Faith Cemetery South, respectively. The name change was announced on Memorial Day 1976, and conflicts arose almost immediately.

Throughout the summer, the name change garnered headlines in the local newspapers and aroused emotional responses from within the Swedish-American community. "Maybe you can do this name changing deal because you figure Swedes don't care," wrote Miss Arden Gustafson in the *Worcester Telegram* on June 10, 1976. "I'm not going to get into this much deeper because I might lose 'my cool,' but here is at least one Swede who cares and is not afraid to stand up and be counted." In many cases, the name change was seen as a repudiation of the Swedish-American community. Stated one letter in the *Worcester Telegram* on August 6 signed by several people, "Among our ancestors, who are buried in both cemeteries, are many who in the past century made real contributions to Worcester's culture and growth… It seems too bad in this bicentennial year, that some of their descendants have felt called upon to deny their roots, and to deny them to the rest of

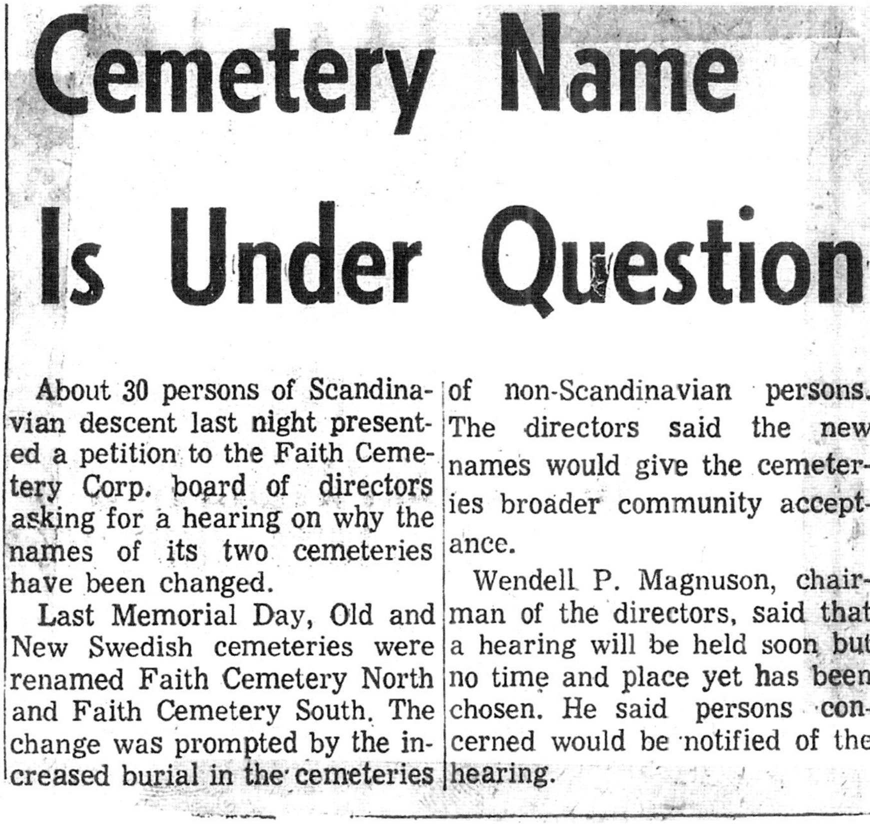

Cemetery Name Is Under Question

About 30 persons of Scandinavian descent last night presented a petition to the Faith Cemetery Corp. board of directors asking for a hearing on why the names of its two cemeteries have been changed.

Last Memorial Day, Old and New Swedish cemeteries were renamed Faith Cemetery North and Faith Cemetery South. The change was prompted by the increased burial in the cemeteries of non-Scandinavian persons. The directors said the new names would give the cemeteries broader community acceptance.

Wendell P. Magnuson, chairman of the directors, said that a hearing will be held soon but no time and place yet has been chosen. He said persons concerned would be notified of the hearing.

The decision to rename the two burial grounds and corporation brought the issue of ethnic identity to the forefront during the summer and fall of 1976. *Author's collection.*

us as well." In a letter to Director Walter Magnusson dated November 30, prominent businessman John Jeppson of the Norton Company noted that the cemetery was established by immigrants who "at considerable sacrifice, raised the funds to establish it." He continued, "Calling it Swedish was not much different from the custom of the English settlers to name places and institutions after people and places in England," and concluded by stating that any name change "would only serve to slight the memory" of both the founders and the Swedish legacy of the area. In September, a petition was sent to the corporation opposing the name change and requesting a special meeting to vote on the matter.

As the controversy continued unabated, it was decided by the directors that a special proxy mailing would be sent out to lot owners to allow for such a vote. On November 10, a letter was sent out stating the position of the corporation and the reasons for its actions. These included mixed marriages and a decline in the sale of lots. It was felt that the increasing ethnic diversity of the internments and subsequent loss of revenue made the designation Swedish Cemetery "less and less acceptable." Interestingly enough, the directors noted that the name change "was proper as it was in the case of the many churches in the area that dropped 'Swedish' from their name years ago." This letter elicited numerous responses both for and against the name change. Prior to this, one writer actually placed the blame on the Swedish-American community itself:

> *People are now signing the attached petition protesting the name change in the cemetery but are still using the Paxton Memorial Park, Hope and Rural Cemeteries.*
>
> *It appears our Swedish people have missed the point and that a petition should be made to back up our Swedish heritage and as "Swedes" use our cemeteries.*
>
> *It is quite clear that if the Swedes did their part the Board of Directors would not have had to make this decision.*[81]

At the special meeting held on December 7 at Trinity Lutheran Church, the directors announced that the corporation would revert to its original name, as would the two burial grounds. This was in response to the results of the vote by lot owners. The results of the vote, however, are interesting. Of the ballots returned, 625 voted in favor of the name change, while 840 called for the restoration of the original designation—certainly no landslide by any means. The results characterized a community at odds with itself over the question of change at the expense of its ethnic identity. The final tally also symbolized that a great many within the community were willing to accept that change without reservation.

A second, less dramatic name change occurred in April 1999. New Swedish Cemetery was renamed "All Faiths," while the names of the original burial ground and of the corporation were retained. "The Board of Directors of Swedish Cemetery Corporation authorized this name change," stated a publicity notice, "to underscore our long and distinguished tradition of meeting the needs of people of all faiths, races and nationalities." This press release was ingenious, for unlike the defensive nature of the 1976 letter, this statement considered the historical aspect of the corporation as an impetus for change. Unlike the controversy surrounding the 1976 decision, the transition from New

The resting place of Robert C. Olson speaks volumes about identity. A Viking ship flanked by industrial devices marks the grave site of the founder and president of the Olson Manufacturing Company. *Author's collection.*

Swedish to All Faiths was completed without incident, illustrating just how the strength of the ethnic affiliation had weakened. Interestingly enough, at least one director and two letter writers proposed that the name change apply only to New Swedish Cemetery during the 1976 controversy.

This name change, the last transitional facet in the history of the corporation, was a business decision. The new name reflects a more mainstream, encompassing corporation, and one based on business realities rather than ethnic ties. The change also reflects the complete transformation of the Swedish-American ethnic community; no longer are people drawn to the cemetery for purely ethnic reasons. However, as we have seen, even before this symbolic change, the corporation had long ceased functioning as a purely ethnic institution.

Despite such transformations, the Swedish legacy is still visible. At Old Swedish Cemetery, now at capacity, both the American and Swedish flags continue to fly side by side, while many tombstones are inscribed in Swedish. Here can be found the resting places of such prominent personalities as Pehr Holmes, former mayor of Worcester and longtime congressman; Reverend Daniel Sörlin, renowned pastor of Swedish Methodism in America; and his colleague, Reverend Victor Witting, whose memorial marker, engraved in Swedish, stands nearby. The memorial marker of the Jeppson family, successful industrialists and community advocates, is situated next to that of C.F. Lybeck, prominent leader of the Swedish-American temperance movement. A memorial to Olaf F. Anderson—who perished at the infamous

Japanese prison camp O'Donnell following the horrific Bataan Death March in 1942—is inscribed on his parent's tombstone. In all, more than ten thousand of the region's Swedish residents and their families reside here.

Its counterpart, now All Faiths Cemetery, is located one mile west on neighboring Island Road. Situated on a flat peninsula of land, the first impression formed by the visitor is one of tranquility. Leesville Pond offers a natural buffer to encroaching development here; although in the distance looms Interstate 290. Here thousands more Swedish-Americans are buried. As one passes through the granite entrance, the memorial stone erected for departed members of the Vasa Order of America can be seen on the right. A memorial stone bordering Leesville Pond also marks a plot set aside for residents of The Lutheran Home. The marker of Andrew Lundborg, one-time owner of the largest Swedish bookstore east of Chicago, is situated near the entrance; as is the marker of Roland Erickson, former Guarantee Bank president and a president of the Swedish-American Chamber of Commerce. In 1976, Erickson was knighted by the Swedish king for his efforts in promoting unity between the two countries.

Ethnic identity has merged with the reality of the business world. The corporation's website notes, "We are immensely proud of our two resting places. The Swedish Cemetery symbolizes the heritage of a proud people and their accomplishments. All Faiths Cemetery is an expansion and continuation of this tradition." Through trial and error, the Swedish Cemetery Corporation has found that ethnic history can be successfully retained within the context of the modern business world. The founders of the cemetery would be proud.

Compassionate Identity: The Worcester Swedish Charitable Association

Of far-reaching importance was the Worcester Swedish Charitable Association (1901). Officially disbanded in 2004, the WSCA was for generations the great provider for the ethnic community. During its heyday, the association oversaw three branch headquarters (Greendale, Belmont Hill and Quinsigamond Village) and employed two full-time caseworkers. This organization, perhaps more than any other, symbolized the benevolent spirit of community. The collection of the WSCA is also a record of a community beset with the social and financial problems that were seldom discussed in self-promotional histories.

At no time were the association's resources more put to the test as during the Great Depression. The annual report for 1931–32 notes, "The demands… have increased tremendously again this year because of the continuance of the depression." During that particular year, 281 families, numbering over 1,000 individuals were aided—the great majority victims of "unemployment or underemployment," which constituted "92% of our applications for aid." So acute was the unemployment situation that many cases were simply turned over to the city's welfare board. In perhaps an attempt to alleviate some of the suffering, a motion was made on July 14, 1932, "that in cases where the people have been in this country not over three years be turned over to the Welfare Department with the idea that they may be sent back to Sweden."

Improving economic conditions by the late 1930s, however, did not lessen the load of the association. The 1939 annual bulletin, for example, took the

BOARD OF DIRECTORS

President, Andrew B. Holmstrom
Vice-President, Roland S. G. Frodigh
Secretary, Helen L. Carlson
Treasurer, Albert Erickson

TRUSTEES

George Forsberg Arthur G. Swanson
Nils Bjork

AUDITORS

Axel Rosenlund Gerhard Becker
E. Hjalmar Nordstrom

DIRECTORS

J. Engelbert Dahlstrom
Oscar W. Engstrand
Astrid Gustafson
G. Adolph Johnson
Rev. A. G. Lund
N. August Pearson
Lillian H. Person
Roy G. A. Petterson
Axel G. Sandberg
Carl G. Sundquist
Paul R. Swan
Otto E. Wicklund

ADVISORS

Social Work, Marjorie J Smith
Real Estate, B. Elmer Petterson

CASEWORKER

Mildred Berquist Grout

★★★★★★★★★★★★★★★★★

ANNUAL REPORT

1942 -- 1943

Worcester Swedish
Charitable Association

★★★★★★★★★★★★★★★★★★★★

Member of Community Chest

The 1942–43 annual report booklet of the Worcester Swedish Charitable Association assumed a patriotic tone as the United States entered World War II. *Author's collection.*

reader through a day in the life of its caseworker. Issues ranging in scope from a runaway child to an abusive husband and financial assistance were detailed. In that year, 147 families were assisted in one form or another. By the time it celebrated its half century of service in 1951, the annual report for that year noted that the association had "changed from financial relief to friendly counseling, helping with marital problems, parent-child relationships and personality adjustments." One 1954 "Thank You" note praised the association for such support, noting, "I feel I never could have carried this burden alone. Mrs. Jones [the caseworker] has been a great comfort to me whenever I felt disturbed a talk with her made things a little brighter and easier to carry on."

Individual needs varied, ranging from educational assistance to clothing, food and relocation. Consider the 1942 case of Mrs. M.H., an eighty-two-year-old widow. Pastor Theodore Palmer of Zion Lutheran sent a letter to the association in November relating that the unfortunate woman lived "in a poorly heated room at 41 Whipple Street…Under the present circumstances, she is not receiving proper food or care…She is penniless." With the association's financial help, the daughter of Mrs. H. was able to move her into the Swedish Lutheran Old People's Home for proper care. This is but one of thousands of cases that the WSCA acted on during its century in existence. During my research, I was surprised to find my relatives listed as those who had received aid from the association.

The annual tradition of delivering Christmas food baskets to needy persons began shortly after the foundation of the society. Records indicate that from the 1920s through the 1940s, more than 100 baskets (and, in some years, 200 baskets) were distributed to needy families every Christmas. These gifts were funded by donations from the local Swedish-American community, with the deficit funded by the association. The contents of the baskets for 1925 included "1 lb. coffee, 1 pkg. sugar, 2 pkgs. rice, 1 pkg. prunes, 1 lb. mixed nuts, 1 glass jelley, Bread—Popcorn…Besides this, pork, potatoes and oranges will be added." In that year, 150 baskets were distributed. Oftentimes, Christmas assistance came in the form of a check or, in later years, a simple flower arrangement to shut-ins or residents of The Lutheran Home. This tradition continued up until the dissolution of the association.

For those in need of assistance, the WSCA was a godsend. Prior to the advent of the governmental welfare system, the spirit of support and aid manifested in the association proved that the ethnic community undertook great strides to take care of its own. The association was also important in disproving one popular historical account: that success followed every

Dear Friend:

With each passing year we feel that the Christmas Fund of the Worcester Swedish Charitable Association is more firmly a custom among us. We all have good reason to be proud of the splendid token of friendship that we have made our Christmas Fund.

On Christmas 1933 you and other friends brought cheer to 241 Swedish homes and brightened the lives of almost a thousand individuals. It was a large family that we remembered.

All of us want to make Christmas a day of rejoicing for others as well as ourselves, and we can only do it through our close cooperation. We are enclosing an addressed envelope and assure you that a contribution will be greatly appreciated.

With best wishes for a Merry Christmas and a Happy New Year.

Cordially yours,

President

A community that helped its own was evident during the association's annual Christmas food basket drive. This 1934 campaign letter stressed the importance of such good works. *Author's collection.*

Swede. In reality, the Swedish-American community suffered from the same ailments as any other.

By 2004, the WSCA had outlived its usefulness, the great majority of Swedish-Americans had entered into the affluent middle class and the burgeoning federal social and welfare programs over the last quarter century had relieved the association of much of its energy. Gone, too, for the most part, was the tight social network of the Swedish community itself. There was simply no need for a "Swedish" welfare organization if there was no

Transfer of the association's scholarship program to the Greater Worcester Community Foundation, December 2001. Association officers John R. Sundquist (left) and Howard A. Safstrom present foundation president and CEO Ann T. Lisi with a $50,000 check. *Author's collection.*

true community to serve. The WSCA, however, maintained its spirit of benevolence to the end. The last of its efforts went into the transferring of its scholarship program, in conjunction with the Swedish National Federation, over to the Greater Worcester Community Foundation, as well as the restoration of the historic Martin Hedmark mural at Zion Lutheran Church. This unique mural harmoniously blends the Swedish and Worcester experiences together and is worth a visit to the church.

CONCLUSION

The creation of a Swedish-American identity within the United States coincided with the transformation of an American national identity. In many respects, the creation of the ethnic identity was influenced by the developing nature of this national identity. The American identity was influenced by political, religious and racial factors. Such factors influenced both the "native" white stock and their immigrant counterparts. Within the context of the latter two facets, the results on the nation's ethnic sphere were dramatic. The original belief that one could be transformed into an American if one adhered to the political beliefs of the nation gave rise to an emerging national identity crisis focusing on religion and race.

Within this context, immigrant groups sought to portray themselves as adhering to "American values." Thus, many ethnic groups created (or overstated) customs, traditions and values that purportedly symbolized the best of their respective cultures. The creators (or ethnic leaders) of these identities were careful to place them within the framework of American society. Thus, it is no surprise, for example, that the promoters of the 1925 Norse-American Centennial celebration sought to represent the Norwegian ethnic community as "loyal citizens whose values were compatible with American ideals, safe, and conflict-free."[82]

All Nordic immigrant groups in America have promoted the Viking legacy, long a staple in the Scandinavian identity. Such promotion goes beyond a colonial past and claims outright "discovery" of the continent. Swedish-American identity construction has also focused on certain historical and symbolic themes. Most notably, the founding of New Sweden along the Delaware River in 1638 has been the focus of a Swedish-American identity since the first large-scale celebration in 1888. Such celebrations have allowed Swedish-Americans to claim a colonial historical past within the United States, thus placing them on par with the early English Puritans. The tercentenary celebrations of 1938 marked a high point in the promotion of a Swedish-American identity in the United States, and Worcester played a part in those celebrations during the visit of members of the royal family.

On July 11 of that year, Prince Bertil of Sweden visited Worcester, where he received a key to the city from Mayor William A. Bennett, toured the Worcester Art Museum and lunched at the Worcester Country Club; he was also presented with an honorary twenty-five-year service pin at the Norton Company. A baseball game scheduled for him at Norton's was rained out, but ten thousand people still turned out to cheer the prince as he spoke to them during the thunderstorm. That evening, Bertil was an honored guest at a traditional Swedish smörgåsbord held at the Jeppson family estate in Brookfield. On July 12, the *Worcester Telegram* quoted Bertil upon receiving his ceremonial key, "Your city should be proud of the contributions of its Swedish-Americans. It is a city that stands for the best qualities of Svensk-Amerika."

Prince Bertil is not the only royal family member to have visited Worcester. Bertil's uncle Prince Wilhelm visited Worcester in 1907. The greeting given the Swedish prince visibly impressed him and is chronicled in the book *gå till Amerika*. Twenty years later, the prince returned and spoke at Mechanics Hall about his adventures in Africa. Bertil's father, Crown Prince Gustaf Adolf, and Princess Louisa toured Worcester in 1926, visiting the Skandia Credit Union, Fairlawn Hospital and the Swedish Lutheran Old People's Home. The crown prince received an honorary degree from Clark University. The couple also attended the Midsummer Festival held in Greendale, of which they were honored guests.

Symbolic ethnicity, the current expression of one's ethnic past, is based on the celebration of an ethnic heritage largely developed during the great Romantic period of the mid- and late nineteenth century. The development of a national Swedish community gave rise to "national" traditions, most notably Midsummer and Lucia. In addition, the peasant culture of an earlier, simpler Sweden was worshipped and gave rise to the colorful folk costumes of today. This creation of a national folk culture was not unique to Sweden but rather had spread throughout Europe during this period. In addition, the twentieth century has seen the popularity of newer symbols such as the Dala

Ethnic participants Harold and Julie Solomon ham it up at a 1997 Vasa Day outing at SAC Park. Who says Swedes don't have a sense of humor? *Author's collection.*

horse, which became popularized as recently as 1939, when it was introduced to American audiences at the New York World's Fair.

Hero worship is another facet in the development of an ethnic identity. For Polish-Americans, the cult surrounding Count Casmir Pulaski and Thaddeus Kosciusko was great enough to warrant the 1910 unveiling of statues in Washington, D.C. Swedish-Americans rallied around the personalities of King Gustavus Adolphus and inventor John Ericsson. While the cult of the warrior king—the "Lion of the North"—has largely subsided, a Minnesota college does bear his name. As for Ericsson, his memorial statue was dedicated in Washington in 1926. A year after this celebration, Swedish-Americans *and* Sweden would claim as their own aviator and inventor Charles Lindbergh, whose solo flight across the Atlantic in May 1927 brought him worldwide fame. Two months after his historic flight, the aviator thrilled Worcester crowds with a flyover of the city. Lindbergh circled the tower of city hall and dropped a message of greetings to the cheering throngs who crowded Main Street for a glimpse of the *Spirit of St. Louis*. Lindbergh would visit the city on several occasions to discuss and secure funding for the experiments of Dr. Robert Goddard of Clark University, considered the father of modern rocketry. Goddard himself had married Esther Kisk, a Worcester Swede. Following his untimely death in 1945 from cancer, she dutifully returned to their Tallawanda Drive home and organized his papers, which were published in 1970.

The industrial development of Worcester attracted a host of immigrant groups to the city. The Irish had been among the first, involved in the various

A 1938 commemorative honors aviator and inventor Charles Lindbergh, whose 1927 flight made him a symbol of Swedish-American pride. Lindbergh's grandfather had been a member of Sweden's parliament. *Author's collection.*

construction aspects of the Blackstone Canal. By the late 1860s, the first small groups of Swedes had settled into the area, but the population grew slowly over the ensuing decade. A period of massive influx began in the 1880s, resulting in the creation of a Swedish organizational network throughout the city. In this period of intense ethnic rivalries, the Swedes' Protestantism "made them 'natural allies' of native-born, middle class Republicans against Irish Catholic Democrats."[83] This symbiotic relationship between the Republican Yankee establishment and the Swedes lasted for more than a generation. As the Scandinavian element faced questions concerning its loyalty during the First World War, Swedish-born Pehr Holmes was elected mayor three times. Such successes highlighted the favored position attained by the Worcester Swedish-Americans. This relationship began to crumble during the 1920s due to the changing social and political spheres in Worcester. Faced with this reality, many Swedes gravitated toward the KKK as a political move. Hence, the period of the 1920s became an era of intense and often violent ethnic rivalries, particularly between the Swedes and Irish, that came to symbolize the social unrest of the 1920s.

The decade also saw the maturing of the Swedish-American community. It was a period of contradictions, for even as the community grew in organizational strength, the roots of its undoing were being laid. Churches initiated the use of the English language, slowly at first and then more rapidly; the Swedish Lutheran Old People's Home signaled the aging of the immigrant generation, while the roots of the exodus from the enclaves had begun, as in the case of Belmont Hill.

By this time, the Swedes had established small communities within the surrounding towns, namely Auburn and Holden; in Shrewsbury and Millbury, smaller pockets existed. A network of suburban organizations, churches and businesses was established that extended the Swedish influence outside the city limits. These initial settlements were established as early as the 1890s, as in Holden, but during the post–World War II period, second- and third-generation Swedes began to leave the traditional Swedish neighborhoods in Worcester to establish themselves in suburban areas populated by Americans of various ethnic backgrounds. Thus began the period of the disintegration of the structural community, as these successive generations began to socialize, worship and reside outside the boundaries of the ethnic community. The "community" was being absorbed. It was noted in 1961 that the accomplishments of area Swedes had "become so completely identified with Worcester itself that not often is it even labeled Swedish. Quite the most revealing and felicitous comment is that the Swedish people are now thoroughly taken for granted in the City of Worcester."[84] But in a sense, is this not what the early spokespersons of the Swedish ethnic community promoted? Were not Swedes synonymous with being good Americans?

Successive generations also began to work outside the traditional industrial sphere that had long characterized the Swedish workforce. By the postwar era, however, the younger Swedish-American generations not only were living outside the ethnic community, but many had also taken up employment in new fields. For second- and third-generation Swedish-Americans, there was a life outside the factory. This transformation coincided with a decline in the area's major source of employment: the manufacturing sector. The loss of city residents, one historian noted, came largely as a result of this declining industrial base. "You had old facilities, along with employers who were looking for cheap labor, so a lot of the firms just left the area. A large number of the traditional industries—the metal trades and the machine shops, for instance—were hit very hard."[85]

As a result, the manufacturing base of the city, which had peaked during the 1940s, began a rapid decline from which it never recovered. By the early 1970s, the landscape of the city was littered with abandoned mill buildings and factory complexes. The massive American Steel complex in Quinsigamond Village closed its doors in 1971, followed by arms manufacturer Harrington and Richardson two years later. Crompton and Knowles, at one time the largest loom manufacturer in the country, left the city in 1980. The industrial age, an era that had supplied the majority of Swedish immigrants in Worcester with their livelihood, had largely faded from view.

As early as 1944, Zeller described the beginnings of a social transformation that would have enormous consequences on the ethnic makeup of Worcester. "The foreign white stock," she stated, "fed more by northwestern Europeans, will increase in number and in tendency to scatter." She continued:

> *They will be less bound to a certain section of the city because of racial ties and economic conditions. To expand this, a change in the type of work followed by the son, grandson, and great-grandson of the Irish or Swedish, or any other, immigrant tends to take them out of the section where their immediate ancestors first settled, and allows them to live in a more desirable, from their point of view, part of the city. This same fate is bound to happen to all who break away from their racial groupings. This coming in contact not only in their business life but in their social life with other nationalities means that a more rapid increase in the mixing of the population will result.*[86]

The transformation Zeller described accelerated during the postwar period, transforming the ethnic, social and economic state of Worcester. The results of this population shift were dramatic. In 1950, the population of Worcester peaked at just over 203,000; within ten years, the population hovered at about 186,000, or a decline of around 9 percent. At the same time, the surrounding nine towns experienced, on average, a 30 percent increase in population.

Thus, social and economic factors that affected the nation as a whole resulted in a rapid transformation of the local Swedish-American community. The breakdown of the industrial base characterized postwar Worcester. As a result, subsequent generations of Swedish-Americans, many now college-educated, sought employment outside the traditional manufacturing sector. Many began to migrate to the suburbs, seeking better conditions than could be found in the aging, declining industrial city of Worcester. Their ascent into the middle-class, suburban lifestyle brought them into contact with people of varying backgrounds. As a result, the second, third and subsequent generations of Swedish-Americans found it unnecessary to remain within the confines of the ethnic neighborhood—and, in many instances, within the community as well.

The transformation of the Swedish-American community is a process that continues to the present. If one were to view the ethnic community in a structural sense, it would appear that assimilation has indeed taken place. Gone are the ethnic enclaves, while the benevolent, social and religious institutions that were established have long ago shed their ethnic cloaks or disappeared altogether. To a large extent, the Swedish language has disappeared completely from the cultural landscape and surviving organizations, except for use in celebratory services. But does the disappearance of the structural community mean the disappearance of ethnic identity?

While few vestiges of the structural community remain, the notion of *being* Swedish-American does exist. Yet this notion has been transformed in the sense that, in large part, there are no large public demonstrations of Swedish-American ethnic pride. Gone are the social, political and ethnic tensions that spawned such grandiose celebrations and ethnic self-promotional campaigns. The Swedish-American in Worcester today is no longer in competition with an ethnic rival—there is no basis for the promotion of ethnicity based on ethnic or class struggle.

The Swedish-American ethnicity today is rather one of symbolic identity. This identity is based on an individual and personal sense of *being*. For third- and fourth-generation Swedish-Americans in Worcester, there is no direct link to Sweden; these generations were born and raised within an American

Modern ethnicity is fluid, and some actively participate in the ethnic community. Here at a 1998 Swedish festival are Joan Orton, Gulla Magnusson and Leif and Siw Kristiansson. *Author's collection.*

context. Why do some proclaim themselves Swedish-American? Simple: they *choose* to do so. These modern-day ethnics also choose what aspects of this identity they wish to celebrate and when they wish to do so.

Thus, the modern-day "bumper sticker Swedes" of today celebrate their ethnicity in a less public, more personal way than their ancestors. The Dala horse still occupies an important place on the shelf, while a miniature Swedish flag can be found tucked in a corner of the room. Somewhere on a wall there hangs an embroidered proverb in the Swedish language, not fully understood but hanging there just the same. An artifact that once belonged to *mormor* or *morfar* is treasured for sentimental reasons. Books relating to the Swedish-American experience may be purchased. One may even become a member of an online group, such as the newly formed "Swedes from Worcester County, Massachusetts" page on Facebook. In this new Internet age, will social media fill a void for those longing to "be Swedish"?

Rapid technological developments and a shifting identity are reasons why the Gift Chalet in Auburn, Massachusetts, closed its doors in 2012 after

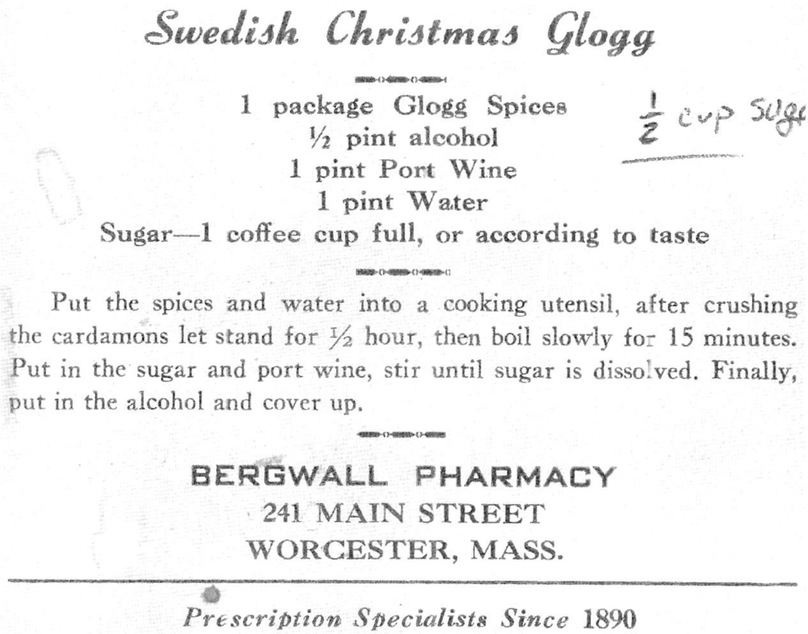

Swedish Christmas Glogg

1 package Glogg Spices
½ pint alcohol
1 pint Port Wine
1 pint Water
Sugar—1 coffee cup full, or according to taste

½ cup Suga

Put the spices and water into a cooking utensil, after crushing the cardamons let stand for ½ hour, then boil slowly for 15 minutes. Put in the sugar and port wine, stir until sugar is dissolved. Finally, put in the alcohol and cover up.

BERGWALL PHARMACY
241 MAIN STREET
WORCESTER, MASS.

Prescription Specialists Since 1890

Many area residents may recall visiting Bergwall Pharmacy for a glass of *glögg* at Christmas. The recipe is seen here on a card handed out to customers. *Author's collection.*

thirty-five years and shifted to online sales only. On February 13, 2013, the *Auburn Daily News* ran an article about the Chalet. Noting that online sales had outpaced sales in its store, President Susan Forsberg Wilkicki remarked, "People only come during Christmas…The old Swedes who were Swedish everyday are gone and the customers we have now are only Swedish in December. We have had to go in other directions to make a living."[87]

The *sil och nykökt potatis* (herring and fresh-cooked potatoes) so instrumental for any outing in Wahlstrom's day is still popular with Swedish-Americans, while *knäckebröd* (hard tack) and Swedish meatballs have become so thoroughly "American" that they are found on supermarket shelves throughout the country. In many Swedish-American households, "*mormor*'s recipes" are still prepared as they were generations ago, thus providing a link to the past. *Janssons Frestelse* (Jansson's Temptation), *inlagda rödbetor* (pickled beets) and *risgrynsgröt* (rice pudding) are foods that have been passed down through the generations. At Christmas, *tomtegubbar* are put out along with the straw goats, while the aroma of potato sausage and *glögg* fill the house. In some cases,

Swedish Bakery Here Flies 1st Shipment to N.Y. Fair

The first of what is expected to be regular shipments of Swedish pastries and breads left the Worcester Airport yesterday for the New York World's Fair.

The Crown Bakery Division of Traditional Products, Inc., Gold Star Boulevard, will supply the delicate, hand - made pastries, the Swedish rye breads and other delicacies for the Swedish Pavillion at the Fair.

John W. Benson, vice president and manager of the Crown division, who was on hand to see the first shipment of 100 pounds of pastries and bread loaded aboard a Northeast Airlines flight said the shipments will be made at least once a week and oftener if the demand is greater.

Lennerton

Crown Bakery consistently wins first place in local polls and is perhaps the last authentic "Swedish" institution in the Worcester area. *Author's collection.*

many recipes have been modified in the process. "Sometimes," noted authors Janet Letnes Martin and Ilene Letnes Lorenz, "America as a 'melting pot' has transferred to the 'cooking pot.'"[88]

The popularity of food as an expression of ethnicity may partially explain why the last true Swedish-American business in Worcester is a bakery. Crown Bakery, established in 1960, has always been Swedish-owned and operated, most notably by the Lundstrom family. Many of the current staff of bakers are Swedish-born. Here one can still purchase Swedish baked goods and special-order traditional Scandinavian favorites. So popular is this institution that the bakery has been honored with numerous local and national awards over the years. It has consistently been voted Worcester's best bakery in polls. In fact, Crown quickly made a name for itself early in its history when it was awarded the contract to supply baked goods for the Swedish Pavilion at the 1964–65 New York World's Fair. Regardless of the strength of an individual's ethnic identification, food is still the great unifier of the modern, translucent ethnic community. This ethnicity is fluid. This ethnicity is constantly changing faces.

Appendix

THE WORCESTER-AREA SWEDES

A Chronology

1868

September 28: Arrival of Carl (Charles) Hanson and his family from Boston. Hanson was born in Uddevalla, province of Bohuslän, and married while in Boston. Hanson is generally regarded as the first recorded Swede to Worcester.

1868–1869

The first group of Swedes arrive in Worcester during this period. Among them are Sven Pålson, Anders Person, Gustaf and Magnus Ahlström, John Vennerström, John Engström, John Jeppson, Philip Styffe, Peter Wärme and the first Swedish woman in the city, Maria Frodigh. Most of these early arrivals came from the Swedish town of Höganäs, province of Skåne.

1869

Male quintet composed of Gustaf Ahlström, John Jeppson, John Engström, Philip Styffe, and O. Wennerström is organized. For a short period, this quintet was associated with the local German musical group Frohsinn.

1871

Scandinavian Literary Organization is established.

1872

April 2: Jennie Pålson becomes the first child born in Worcester to Swedish parents.

1873
March 10: Carl Hanson establishes the Swedish and Norwegian National Singing Club.
Scandinavian Literary Organization is dissolved.

1878
October 13: The First Swedish Methodist Episcopal Church in Quinsigamond Village is organized. This was the first Swedish congregation in Worcester and the first Swedish Methodist congregation in New England.

1880
March 6: Nordstjernan Sick Benefit and Temperance Society is organized.
August 25: The Swedish Evangelical Free Church of Worcester is organized. By 1885, the church had affiliated with the Congregationalists and became known as the First Swedish Evangelical Congregational Church.
November 17: First Swedish Baptist Church is organized.

1881
February 26: The Viking Council of the Independent Order of Mystic Brothers is established.
August 2: Swedish Evangelical Lutheran Gethsemane Church is organized.

1883–1885
Kalender öfver Svenarkarne I Worcester is published by Zetterman and Lätt. This early address book listed the names of Worcester's Swedish residents.
Nord-Östern (the *Northeast*), the first Swedish newspaper in Worcester, is published.

1884
March 30: First Swedish Methodist Episcopal Church on Stebbins Street in Quinsigamond Village is dedicated (currently Quinsigamond Methodist Church).
May 30: First Swedish Baptist Church on Mulberry Street is dedicated.

1885
January 25: First Swedish Evangelical Congregational Church on Providence Street is dedicated.
April 9: Second Swedish Methodist Episcopal Church is organized.

August: Church building on Thomas Street is purchased by the Second Swedish Methodist Episcopal Church (the congregation became popularly known as the Thomas Street Methodist Church).
November 21: The Swedish Cemetery Corporation votes to purchase three acres on Webster Street for use as a burial ground.

1886
Memorial Day: The Swedish Cemetery on Webster Street is officially dedicated with elaborate ceremonies; burials had been ongoing.
August 21: The Swedish-American newspaper *Worcester Veckoblad* is established. The following year, the name changed to *Skandinavia*.
September 26: The Swedish Evangelical Lutheran Gethsemane Church on Mulberry Street is dedicated.

1888
February 28: Svea Gille Association is organized. The association quickly became the premier Swedish social organization in the Worcester area.
Lyran, a double male quartet, is established.

1888–1889
Fosterlandet is published.

1890
Swedish Publishing Company is incorporated.

1891
February 3: Salvation Army Quinsigamond No. 2 Corps is organized as a Swedish speaking corps.
March 8: Svea Council (for women) of the Independent Order of Mystic Brothers is established.
December 20: Monitor Lodge IOGT is established.
The First Swedish Congregational Church establishes a chapel in Quinsigamond Village.
Quinsigamonds Väl Lodge IOGT is established.

1892
February 14: Swedish Gymnastic Club is organized.
February 28: A joint IOGT Sick Benefit Association is formed.
The Swedish Christian Workers Association of Chaffins in Holden is organized.

1893

October: Salvation Army Worcester No. 3 Corps is organized as the second Swedish-speaking corps.
December: Brage Male Chorus is organized as a member of the American Union of Swedish Singers (AUSS).
First Swedish Methodist Episcopal Church is enlarged.
Neptune Male Chorus is organized.
The Scandinavian Workers' Club Trade Union is established (Socialist).

1894

May: The Svea Gille Association clubhouse along the Shrewsbury side of Lake Quinsigamond is dedicated.
September: Viking Bicycle Club is organized. The club brought together Swedes interested in the bicycle craze that swept America.
October 21: The Second Swedish Congregational Church is organized in Quinsigamond Village (currently Bethlehem Covenant Church).
December 8: Huge festival is held at Mechanics Hall to celebrate the 400th anniversary of the birth of Gustavus II Adolphus. The king's death on a German battlefield assured him a place in Swedish national history. The Gustavus Adolphus Festival was held annually for over twenty years.

1894–1895

Dundret is published.
Blixten is published.
Swedish Herald is published.

1895

October 11: Ankaret Lodge IOGT is organized.
Swedish American Republican Club of Ward 2 is organized.
Swedish Christian Workers Association dedicates its Holden chapel.

1895–1896

Östra Sändebundet is published.
Östra Vecko-Posten is published.

1896

February 20: Viking Lodge, Knights of Honor, is established. The organization aided members in time of sickness or death.
April 18: The Second Swedish Baptist Church is organized.

June 4: The First Swedish Evangelical Congregational Church dedicates its new quarters, a former American Congregational church at Salem Square (became popularly known as the Salem Square Congregational Church).
July 26: Swedish Evangelical Lutheran Emanuel Church is organized (currently Emanuel Lutheran Church).
November 8: The Second Swedish Baptist congregation dedicates its new church on Harlem Street.
Österns Veckoblad begins publication.

1896–1897
Gladt Humor is published.

1896–1898
Svensk-Amerikanska Affärskalendern för År 1896 is published by the Swedish Publishing Company. This almanac included information on the city's Swedish residents, churches and businesses. It also listed Swedish contacts in Boston.
IOGT Camp Association hosts a summer campground at Natural History Park along the Worcester shore of Lake Quinsigamond.
Kyrkotidningen is published.
Arbetarens Vän is published.

1897
April 27: Count Englebrect No. 131 of the Foresters of America is established.
Swedish Engineers Society is organized. Swedish birth, a technical education and a noteworthy engineering achievement were among the requirements of the organization.
The Swedish-American newspaper *Svea* is established by Hans Trulson.

1898
January 7: Egalite social organization is established.
April 3: Ragnar Lodge No. 10 of the Vasa Order of America becomes the first established lodge of the VOA in Worcester.
November 18: Cornerstone is laid for the Swedish Evangelical Lutheran Emanuel Church.
Svenskarne i Worcester, 1868–1898 (*The Swedes in Worcester, 1868–1898*), a thirty-year historical retrospective on the Swedish-American community, is written by Hjalmar Nilsson and Eric Knutson. The book was published by Skandinavias Bok och Tidningstryckeri (Scandinavia Book and Newspaper Printing Company).

1898–1901
Nya Fäderneslandet is published.

1899
April 4: Flora Lodge No. 15 VOA (for Swedish women) is established.
November 19: Swedish Evangelical Lutheran Emanuel Church on Greenwood Street is dedicated.
Second Swedish Congregational Church on Greenwood Street is completed.

1900
August 29: John Ericsson No. 25 VOA is established.
Engelbrekt Club is organized; eventually, a clubhouse along the Worcester shoreline of Lake Quinsigamond was constructed.

1901
February 16: The Worcester Swedish Charitable Association is organized. In time, the WSCA became the area's foremost Swedish charitable organization, with branches throughout the city.
March 2: Aurora Society (Swedish women only) is organized. The society's goal was to assist members in sickness and to contribute toward a member's funeral expense.
Quinsigamond Salvation Army building is constructed on Greenwood Street.
Swedish Christian Sick and Benefit Society is established.
Ankaret Lodge No. 15 IOGT disbands.

1902
February 26: Aurora Society (for women) is affiliated with the Foresters of America.
May 11: Scandinavian Methodist Episcopal Mission is organized. This congregation was established by Chresten Peterson out of classes held at the Thomas Street Methodist Church (now Epworth).
May 21: Victoria Lodge No. 43 VOA (for Swedish women) is established.
Carl XV Lodge No. 45 of the Scandinavian Fraternity of America becomes first SFA lodge established in Worcester.
Eagle Lodge IOGT is established.

1902–1907
Skandinaviske Missionären is published.

1903

November: The Swedish Christian Workers Association of Chaffins is incorporated as the Scandinavian Evangelical Congregational Church of Holden, Massachusetts.

1904

Skandinavisk Adresskalendar öfver Worcester, Massachusetts is published by Thure Hanson. This address book contained the names of the city's Swedish, Norwegian, Danish and Finnish residents, churches and organizations.
February 9: Höganäs Föreningen (the Höganäs Society) is organized. Membership was limited to Höganäs-area natives and their descendants.
April 23: Queen Louise Lodge No. 57 of the SFA is established.
Worcester Swedish Charitable Association is incorporated under Massachusetts law.

1905

Swedish American Republican Club of Ward 1 is organized.
Swedish American Republican Club of Ward 6 is organized.
Monitor Lodge No. 3 IOGT disbands.
Thule Building is constructed for the Thule Hall Music Association at 184 Main Street. The building became a meeting place for many local Swedish-American organizations.

1905–1908

Församlingens-Posten is published.

1906

March 4: Kämpen Lodge No. 15 IOGT is established.
Swedish American Republican Clubs in Wards 1, 2 and 6 are combined to form the Swedish American Republican League of Worcester.

1906–1908

Missionären is published.

1907

Skandinavisk Adresskalendar öfver Worcester, Massachusetts is again published by Thure Hanson. This address book contained the names of the city's Swedish, Norwegian, Danish and Finnish residents, churches and organizations.

August 26: Visit of Prince Wilhelm of Sweden to Worcester takes place. A sixty-foot-high archway modeled after Norrebro Port (a sixteenth-century northern gateway to Stockholm's Gamla Stan) is erected over Front Street in honor of the Prince. Thousands turn out to greet him.
Thule Male Chorus is organized.
Vestry of the new First Swedish Baptist Church on Belmont Street is constructed.

1907–1910
Reformatoren is published.

1908
February 18: The Daughters of the North, an independent ladies' lodge, is established.
Spring: Svenska-Amerikanska Förbundet is organized.
Hvita Bandet begins publication.

1909
November 5: The Viking Guards, the only independent Swedish military organization in America, is organized.
Swedish American Republican Clubs are organized in Wards 3, 4 and 8.

1910
Swedish-American Souvenir is published by Thure Hanson. This booklet gave an historical overview of the Swedes in Worcester, as well as the current status of the community, highlighting churches, organizations and prominent residents.
April 27: Gustaf V Lodge No. 118 SFA is organized.
August 2: Cornerstone is laid for new Swedish Evangelical Lutheran Gethsemane Church.
November: Swedish Evangelical Lutheran Gethsemane Church on Belmont Street is dedicated.
Swedish Cemetery is enlarged.

1911
June 12: Svenska-Amerikanska Förbundet is reorganized into Svenska Nationalförbundet (the Swedish National Federation).
September 11: Progress Lodge No. 128 SFA is organized.
November 11: The new First Lutheran Church is dedicated on Belmont Street. The church was constructed out of granite taken from the city's first Union Station, which had been in the process of being demolished.
Morgonstjärnan Lodge No. 16 IOGT is established.

1912
March 28–April 8: Dedication ceremonies are held for new First Swedish Baptist Church on Belmont Street.
June: The Swedish National Federation hosts a Swedish National Day, replete with Midsummer celebrations and parade that attracted thousands.
Completed First Swedish Baptist Church on Belmont Street is dedicated.
Kärnan Lodge No. 147 SFA is established.

1913
Swedish Cemetery is enlarged.
Vårblomman Lodge No. 150 SFA is organized.

1914
October 21: Evangelical Lutheran Zion Church is organized (it becomes Zion Lutheran Church). It is popularly known as Greendale Lutheran Church.
Swedish Cemetery is enlarged.

1915
First Swedish Methodist Episcopal Church is enlarged.

1916
January 1: Skandia Credit Union opens for business.
October 22: Vestry of Zion Lutheran Church is dedicated.
John Jeppson is knighted by the king of Sweden (Royal Order of Vasa, Knight First Class).

1917
Swedish Cemetery is enlarged.
Swedish Evangelical Lutheran Gethsemane Church is renamed First Lutheran Church.

1917–1920
Swedish-born Pehr Holmes serves as mayor of Worcester. He was also founder and owner of Holmes Electrotype.

1918
Svea buys out *Skandinavia*, and the two papers merge under the *Svea* banner.

1919
Eagle Lodge No. 4 IOGT is disbanded.

1920
January 30: Scandinavian Women's Gymnastic Club is organized.
April 27: Mendelssohn Singers is organized. This popular all-male chorus stressed sacred and classical music in its repertoire.
May 5: The Viking Guards vote to disband and affiliate with the Scandinavian Fraternity of America as Viking Lodge.
May 17: New England Lutheran Conference votes to establish a home for the aged in Worcester. The former Goulding Estate on Harvard Street is purchased with assistance from the Jeppson family and dedicated as the Swedish Lutheran Old People's Home.
June 16: Nobel Lodge No. 383 VOA is established.
July 6: Englebrect Society affiliates with the Vasa Order of America as Englebrect Lodge No. 384.
July 11: Completed Zion (Greendale) Lutheran Church is dedicated.

1921
January 27: Calvary Lutheran Church is organized as the first English-speaking Lutheran congregation in city.
March 7: Proposed Swedish hospital is discussed at a meeting of the Swedish National Federation.
June 20: Scandinavian Societies Building Association is organized in an effort to find a permanent home for the city's numerous Scandinavian organizations.
June 24: Fairlawn Hospital is incorporated. The former Norcross estate on May Street is purchased by soliciting funds throughout the Swedish-American community.
July 19: The Daughters of the North affiliate with the Vasa Order of America as Dottrar av Norden No. 398.
July 30: Viking and Svea Councils of the Independent Order of Mystic Brothers merge and affiliate with the Vasa Order of America as Sveaborg Lodge No. 400.
The Odin Club is organized. The membership was composed of prominent Swedish-American businessmen and professionals.
A tract of land surrounded by Leesville Pond is purchased by the Swedish Cemetery Corporation and named New Swedish Cemetery. The State of Massachusetts amends the Auburn-Worcester line, thereby placing the burial ground entirely within Worcester city limits.

Skogsblomman Society of Auburn is organized.
Unity Lodge No. 4 IOGT is established.

1922

February 7: Vasa Committee, the unifying body of local Vasa lodges, is established. The committee was composed of three delegates from each of the local lodges in Worcester.
June 11: Fairlawn Hospital is opened to the public after extensive remodeling of the former Norcross estate.
July 2: New Swedish Cemetery is formally opened.

1923

Skandinaviska Gymnastik och Idrottsklubben is established (becomes the Scandinavian Athletic Club, popularly known as SAC).

1924

July: Salvation Army Corps No. 4, the Finnish corps located on Belmont Hill, is transferred to Greendale and reorganizes as a Swedish speaking corps.
November 14: Sunderland Road Chapel is dedicated by First Swedish Baptist Church. The chapel served church members living in immediate neighborhood.
December: Bethel Lutheran congregation of Auburn holds first worship services in basement of the uncompleted church.
A new eight-acre playground on Plantation Street is dedicated as Holmes Field in recognition of the efforts made by Pehr Holmes to secure the land.
Unity Lodge No. 4 IOGT is disbanded.

1924–1930

Pehr Holmes serves on the Governor's Council of Massachusetts.

1925

May 3: Cornerstone of Calvary Lutheran Church on Salisbury Street is laid.
October 4: Calvary Lutheran Church parsonage and parish house are dedicated at Salisbury and Wachusett Streets.
November 18: Swedish Lutheran Old People's Home addition is dedicated.

1926

June 17: Crown Prince Gustav Adolf and his wife tour Worcester. The crown prince receives an honorary degree from Clark University. The Royal Couple

also tour the Swedish Lutheran Old People's Home and Fairlawn Hospital and attend the huge Midsummer Festival at the Agricultural Fairgrounds in Greendale, where thousands turn out to greet them.
July: The Scandinavian Peoples' Park Association, a subsidiary of the Scandinavian Workers' Club Trade Union, dedicates its new summer quarters at Trowbridgeville Lake in Auburn.
September 26: The former Governor Davis Mansion at 89 Lincoln Street is dedicated as the new headquarters for the city's numerous Scandinavian organizations. This meeting place was under the jurisdiction of the Scandinavian Societies Building Association Inc., later known as Lincoln Associates. Member groups were stockholders in the corporation.

1927
January: Prince Wilhelm visits Worcester for a second time. Wilhelm lectures at Mechanics Hall about his hunting experiences in Africa. He gives two talks, one in English and the other in Swedish.
June 19: The new Epworth Swedish Methodist Church on Salisbury Street is dedicated. This church replaced the edifice on Thomas Street.
July 22: Charles Lindbergh flies over the city and, circling city hall, drops a formal greeting as thousands cheer.
October 28: First Lutheran Church Parish House is formally dedicated.
November 27: First Swedish Methodist Episcopal Church addition is dedicated. Thule Male Chorus performs at the John Ericsson Memorial dedication in Washington, D.C., and for Calvin Coolidge at the White House.

1928
February 20: The first commercial telephone call from the United States to Sweden takes place from Worcester. *Telegram and Gazette* editor George Booth and pastor John Eckstrom called Archbishop Nathan Söderblom in Uppsala. The three-minute call totaled $81.75.
July 2: Quinsigamond Lodge No. 517 VOA is organized.
July: The Scandinavian People's Park Association (a subsidiary of the Scandinavian Worker's Educational Association Inc.) officially opens its new clubhouse and pavilion at the People's Park on Trowbridgeville Lake in Auburn.
August 17: The Scandinavian Athletic Club (SAC) purchases a cottage and seven acres on Lake Avenue in Shrewsbury.
October 28: Charles Lindbergh Lodge No. 520 VOA is organized in Auburn.

November 1: The *Worcester Evening Post* publishes a work entitled "The History of the Swedish People in Worcester and Worcester County" to commemorate sixty years of Swedish settlement in the area.
Immanuel Lutheran congregation is organized in Holden.

1929
February 7: Worcester native Captain George Fried and his wife visit the city as guests of the Jeppsons. Fried and his wife were feted at a public reception and presented with gifts from the city and the Italian-American community for his role in several rescues at sea, including the Italian ship *Florida*. A commemorative plaque honoring Captain Fried today hangs in Trinity Lutheran Church.
March 25–26: Captain Einar Lundborg of the Swedish Royal Air Force and his wife visit Worcester as guests of the Jeppsons. Captain Lundborg receives a key to the city from Mayor O'Hara, and more than 1,200 people turn out to hear a lecture given by the famous flying ace.
April 6: Harmoni Lodge No. 529 VOA (Swedish women) is organized.
Spring–Summer: A summer clubhouse featuring a unique domed ceiling is erected for the Scandinavian Athletic Club.
August 18: Kämpen Lodge IOGT clubhouse at Sears Island is dedicated.
December 31: Skandia Credit Union is granted a banking charter by state.
SAC Ladies Auxiliary is organized.
Plot of land at New Swedish Cemetery is laid out for use by Swedish Lutheran Old People's Home.
Immanuel Lutheran Church in Holden is erected.
Bethel Lutheran Church in Auburn is completed.

1930
January 25: Famous Swedish sculptor Carl Milles visits the Worcester Art Museum on his first U.S. tour.
April 1: A remodeled Skandia Bank and Trust Company is opened to the public in the Slater Building Arcade.

1931–1947
Pehr Holmes serves the Fourth Congressional District as a member of the House of Representatives.

1934
Skandia Bank and Trust Company becomes Guarantee Bank and Trust Company.

1938

Swedish-American Tercentenary Year

May 31: The *Worcester Evening Post* publishes a work entitled "The History of the Swedish People in Worcester and Worcester County" to commemorate the tercentenary.

June 5: Worcester celebrates 300th anniversary of the founding of the New Sweden colony in Delaware with elaborate exercises at Worcester Memorial Auditorium that honor the local Swedish-American community. A chorus of more than five hundred Swedish singers perform at the Auditorium under the direction of Carl Dramstad of Stockholm. This concert is broadcast to Sweden.

July 11: Prince Bertil of Sweden visits Worcester in connection with the tercentenary celebration. The prince tours the Worcester Art Museum, lunches at the Worcester Country Club and is presented with a key to the city by Mayor William Bennett. Despite a heavy thunderstorm, more than ten thousand spectators turn out at the Norton Company Fairgrounds to greet him.

1939

November 25: Nordic Lodge No. 611 VOA is organized as the area's first English-speaking Vasa lodge.

1940

November 13: Harmoni Lodge No. 529 VOA merges with Quinsigamond Lodge No. 517.

1941

January 28: Swedish Folkdance Club is organized.

May: Popular Swedish singer Harry Brandelius performs at the Hotel Bancroft in Worcester as a guest of Nordic Lodge No. 611 VOA. Brandelius also performs live at radio station WTAG.

November: The Scandinavian Ski Club is organized.

George Jeppson of the Norton Company donates the family home at 1 Drury Lane to Worcester Polytechnic Institute (WPI) as a memorial to his parents.

Epworth Swedish Methodist Church is renamed Epworth Methodist Church.

1943

January: First Swedish Baptist Church officially becomes Belmont Street Baptist Church.

1945

Töreboda Club is organized. Membership was limited to those from the Västergotland province of Sweden. This organization met biannually for gatherings.

Logen Döttrar av Norden No. 398 VOA Anglicized its name to Daughters of the North Lodge No. 398.

1946

Our Viking Industrialists is published by Svea. This 245-page book highlighted Swedish-American businesses in the Greater Worcester area and New England.

1947

Bethlehem Congregational (formerly Second Swedish Congregational) Church joins the Covenant Church of America and becomes Bethlehem Covenant Church.

The Scandinavian Evangelical Congregational Church of Holden changes its name to Chaffins Congregational Church.

Astra USA, a subsidiary of Swedish company Astra Pharmaceuticals, begins U.S. operations in Greendale.

1948

January 1: First Lutheran (Swedish), Bethany Lutheran (Swedish-Finnish) and Calvary Lutheran (American) combine to form the new Trinity Lutheran Church congregation. Worship services were held at First Lutheran on Belmont Street pending the completion of the new Trinity Lutheran Church.

May 23: Archbishop Erling Eidem from Sweden officiates at the groundbreaking for Zion Lutheran Church Parish House. Later that day, the altar cloth embroidered by Sweden's King Gustaf V is dedicated in an elaborate ceremony at First Lutheran Church. Guests include Swedish Archbishop Erling Eidem and Reverend Karl E. Mattson, president of the New England Lutheran Conference.

July 5: A crowd of more than 7,500 attends a Swedish sports program sponsored by the Scandinavian Athletic Club. Held at WPI, highlights include a soccer game featuring Djurgården I.F. soccer team and the famous Sophia Girls gymnastics group, both from Stockholm. Each group receives a key to the city of Worcester.

July 11: Three hundred people attend the dedication of the Greendale War Memorial, designed by Swedish-American sculptor Carl Milles and made out of black granite from Sweden. The Greendale American

Legion Post 319 sponsored the piece with assistance from George Jeppson of Norton Company.
November: Cornerstone is laid for the new Immanuel Lutheran Church in Holden. The church was built from materials of the former Calvary Lutheran Church in Worcester, which was dismantled to make way for Trinity Lutheran Church. In effect, Immanuel Lutheran is a modified version of Calvary Lutheran.

1949
October 9: The new Immanuel Lutheran Church in Holden is dedicated.
The Salem Square Congregational Church joins the Evangelical Mission Covenant Church of America and becomes Salem Square Covenant Church.

1950
January 14: Nobel Lodge No. 383 VOA merges with Ragnar Lodge No. 10.

1950–1953
Andrew Holmstrom serves as first mayor of Worcester under the new city charter. Holmstrom was also a vice-president at the Norton Company.

1951–1952
Bethlehem Covenant Church is remodeled and enlarged.

1952
June 1: New Trinity Lutheran Church at Salisbury and Lancaster Streets is officially consecrated.

1955
The *SAC Party* dance program hosted by Paul Larson begins airing over radio station WORC. Hosted live from the Dome Room at SAC Park, it featured Swedish-American accordionist Nils Lundin and his orchestra. This Saturday night staple remained on the air for more than twenty years.
Fairlawn Hospital addition is completed.

1956
December 6: Scandinavian Women's Gymnastics Club is reorganized and incorporated as the Scandinavian Women's Club.

1957

February 27: Engelbrekt Lodge No. 384 (men's lodge) VOA merges with Quinsigamond Lodge No. 517.

1958

October 18: More than five hundred delegates from the Bay State Historical League gather in joint session with the Worcester Historical Society. The daylong event celebrated "The Culture and Contribution of the Swedish People to Worcester."
November 2: Cornerstone is laid for new Bethel Lutheran Church in Auburn.

1959

February 11: Flora Lodge No. 15 VOA (women's lodge) and Sveaborg Lodge No. 400 VOA merge with Quinsigamond Lodge No. 517.
August 2: New Bethel Lutheran Church in Auburn is dedicated.

1960

July 29: Daughters of the North Lodge No. 398 VOA is amalgamated with Charles Lindbergh Lodge No. 520.
Crown Bakery opens on Gold Star Boulevard.

1961

April 20: Number 89 Lincoln Street, lodge home to the city's Scandinavian-American organizations, is evacuated per order of the state. The construction of I-290 forced its demolition.

1962

Fall: Fairlawn Hospital addition is completed.

1964–1965

Crown Bakery supplies baked goods to the Swedish Pavilion at the New York World's Fair.

1965

Memorial Day: The Four Apostles memorial monument is dedicated at New Swedish Cemetery. The monument weighs seventy-three thousand pounds and stands eighteen feet tall. A hidden carillon at the top plays music at programmed times.

1967

September 30: The Vasa Memorial Stone is dedicated at New Swedish Cemetery, while Quinsigamond Lodge No. 517 VOA dedicates the former IOGT Hall on Ekman Street as Vasa Hall. The hall became a meeting place for area Vasa lodges and events.

1969

The new Salem Covenant Church on East Mountain Street is dedicated. Construction of the Worcester Center Galleria shopping mall forced the demolition of the old church.

1971

October 11: Jularbogille, a fifty-member accordion group, and Swedish singer Bertil Boo tour Worcester and perform at SAC Park. The visit was part of a larger New England tour. A documentary of this tour ran for several years on Swedish television. Footage included the group touring Worcester, receiving a key to the city and performing at SAC, as well as and interviews with a few Worcester-area Swedes.

1972

June 4: Scandinavian Athletic Club unveils its newly renovated clubhouse. The clubhouse became a year-round recreational facility.

1973

February: Noah's Ark, a sculpture by well-known Swedish artist Åke Holm, is presented to Worcester by the Town of Höganäs, Sweden. Despite a search by this author, the whereabouts of the sculpture remain unknown.
Memorial Day: By director's vote, the Swedish Cemetery Corporation is renamed Faith Cemetery Corporation, and the names of the two cemeteries are changed to Faith Cemetery North and Faith Cemetery South.
December 7: Cemetery lot owners vote against the new name change, and the corporation concedes. Out of 1,913 ballots mailed, 620 voted for the name change and 836 against.
Engelbrekt Club sells its Lake Avenue property to the Marine Corps League.
Roland Erickson is knighted by the king of Sweden (Commander, Royal Order of the North Star).

1977

The Conifer Group, parent company of Guarantee Bank, phases out the Viking Ship symbol, in use since 1930.

1979

May 20: The Lutheran Home addition is dedicated. The new wing is named after the late Reverend O. Karl Olander, former pastor of Trinity Lutheran Church.

1980

May 20: Victoria Lodge No. 43 VOA merges with John Ericsson Lodge No. 25.

1981

Astra USA constructs a new headquarters in Westborough, Massachusetts, and moves out of Worcester.

1984

May 23: Ragnar Lodge No. 10 VOA merges with Quinsigamond Lodge No. 517.

1986

John Anderson serves as mayor of Worcester.

1987

June: Alice Carlson of Millbury, formerly of Worcester, is named Swedish-American of the Year. Elaborate ceremonies take place in Sweden over the summer. Carlson visits with King Carl XVI Gustav and Queen Sylvia.
November 23: Guarantee Bank becomes Bank of New England–Worcester following the sale of the Conifer Group to Bank of New England.
Fairlawn Hospital is closed and renovated into a rehabilitation facility known as Fairlawn Rehabilitation. Stockholders, including the Swedish National Federation, are paid off through the sale of stock.

1992

November 8: Charles Lindbergh Lodge No. 520 VOA is dissolved.

1993–1994

October 3–March 31: The 125th anniversary of the Swedish presence in Worcester is celebrated in the exhibit *gå till Amerika* at the Worcester Historical Museum. Community events include a Swedish film festival; a Lucia celebration held at Trinity Lutheran Church; a visit by Reverend Henrik Svenungsson, the bishop of Stockholm; and a public symposium that attracted speakers from across the country and Sweden. A book by the same name is published.

1994

Quinsigamond Lodge No. 517 sells Vasa Hall.
SARA (Swedish Ancestry Research Association) is organized to help persons trace their Swedish roots.

1998

September: During Worcester's 150th anniversary celebration as a city, a two-week celebration highlighting the city's Swedish-American culture and history is held at the Mount Carmel Church center.
The Swedish National Federation discontinues its annual Midsummer Festival.

1999

April: New Swedish Cemetery is renamed All Faiths Cemetery by the Swedish Cemetery Corporation. The corporation and the Old Swedish Cemetery retain their respective names.
December 12: Nordic Lodge No. 611 VOA and Immanuel Lutheran Church sponsors a joint Lucia Festival at the church.

2000

June 22: The amateur Swedish theater group Norabygdens Teatersällskap performs its historical play *Bishop Hill-spelet* at Trinity Lutheran Church for a crowd of about 125 persons.

2001

November: The Scandinavian Festival and Lucia are held at SAC Park and enjoyed by almost four hundred attendees. The event marked the first large-scale Lucia celebration in almost a decade.

2002

January: In a joint effort, the Swedish National Federation and the Worcester Swedish Charitable Association transfer the management of their scholarship funds over to the Greater Worcester Community Foundation.
June: The Swedish National Federation revives its annual Midsummer Festival.
The Arcadia pictorial history *Swedes of Greater Worcester* is published.

2003

The Swedish National Federation celebrates its centennial. A short history of the organization is privately published.

Fall: Worcester Swedish Charitable Association is disbanded. The association's final contribution funds the restoration of the historic Martin Hedmark mural located in the chapel of Zion Lutheran Church.
October 10–13: Nordic Heritage Trust cosponsors the annual meeting of the Swedish American Historical Society, a national organization based in Chicago. The three-day affair includes guest speakers, tours of Swedish-American sites and a Scandinavian dinner dance sponsored by Nordic Lodge No. 611 VOA.
December 30: A box of historical materials relating to Swedish Worcester is sent to the *Emigrantintitutet* (House of Emigrants) in Växjö, Sweden, courtesy of the Swedish National Federation.

2005
The Arcadia pictorial history *Swedes of Greater Worcester Revisited* is published.

2006
February 26: Quinsigamond Corps of the Salvation Army holds the last service in its quarters on Millbury Street. The corps was later decommissioned.

2009
Scandinavian Women's Club is disbanded.

2010
May 8: John Ericsson Lodge No. 25 VOA is disbanded.

2011
November 16: Quinsigamond Lodge No. 517 VOA is disbanded.

2012
Sheehan Health Group takes over The Lutheran Home from Lutheran Social Services and renames the facility Lutheran Rehabilitation and Skilled Care Center.

2014
Nordic Lodge No. 611 VOA celebrates its seventy-fifth anniversary. It remains the sole Vasa lodge in the Greater Worcester area.

2015

Facebook page "Swedes from Worcester County, Massachusetts" is established.

The book *Swedish Heritage of Greater Worcester* is published by The History Press.

The information presented here represents the most comprehensive timeline of Swedish Worcester published. The author assumes responsibility for any omissions or factual inconsistencies.

NOTES

Introduction

1. Barton, *Letters from the Promised Land*, 20.
2. Ljungmark, *Swedish Exodus*, 91.
3. Barton, *Folk Divided*, 4.
4. Nutt, *History of Worcester and Its People*, 351.

Chapter 1

5. Pierson, *Tale of Two Worcesters*, 79.
6. Salvatore, *We All Got History*, 98.
7. Worcester Board of Trade, *Tribute to the Columbian Year*, 7.
8. Rice, *Worcester of Eighteen Hundred and Ninety-Eight*, 5.
9. Kolesar, "Worcester Swedes Entered."
10. Estus and McClymer, *gå till Amerika*, 3.
11. Spear, *Worcester's Three-Deckers*, 5.
12. Tulloch, *Worcester*, 11.
13. Harvey, "First Swede in Worcester," 75.
14. Estus and McClymer, *gå till Amerika*, 36.
15. Westman and Johnson, "Swedish Methodism in America," *Swedish Element in the United States*, 2:4, 113.
16. Zetterman and Lätt, "Author's Forward," *Kalender Öfver Svenskarne i Worcester*.
17. Conzen, "Immigrants, Immigrant Neighborhoods, and Ethnic Identity," 610.
18. Hanson, *Swedish-American Souvenir*, 1.
19. *Worcester Evening Post*, June 17, 1926.

20. Tymeson, "Hinge that Opened the Gate," 3.
21. *Svea*, "Swedish-Americans in Worcester," June 14, 1922.
22. Balk, "Expansion of Worcester and Its Affect on the Surrounding Towns."
23. Creveling, "Patterns of Cultural Groups in Worcester."
24. *Historical Sketch of Auburn*, 4, compiled by the Federal Writers' Project of the WPA, Massachusetts, 1937.
25. *Evening Gazette*, May 4, 1926.
26. Balk, "Expansion of Worcester and Its Affect on the Surrounding Towns," 159.
27. Westman and Johnson, "Worcester, Massachusetts, and Its Swedish-American Population," *Swedish Element in the United States*, vol. 1, 382.
28. *Worcester Daily Telegram*, July 25, 1928.

Chapter 2

29. *Svea*, April 16, 1959.
30. Andreen, *Det Svenska Språket i Amerika*, 18.
31. Karlson, "Swedish Population of Worcester," 31.
32. Barton, *Folk Divided*, 306.
33. Steinberg, *Ethnic Myth*, 57.
34. Waters, *Ethnic Options*, 164.

Chapter 3

35. Kolesar, "Worcester Swedes Entered," 41.
36. Moynihan, "Swedes and Yankees in Worcester Politics," 23.
37. Kolesar, "Worcester Swedes Entered."
38. Estus and McClymer, *gå till Amerika*, 107.
39. Ibid., 110.
40. Rosenzweig, *Eight Hours for What We Will*, 126.
41. John McClymer, "Passing from Light into Dark," Assumption College, www.assumption.edu/ahc/1920s/passingrevisedversion.html.
42. Gerstle, "Liberty, Coercion, and the Making of Americans," 527.
43. Karlson, "Swedish Population in Worcester," 2.

Chapter 4

44. Blanck, *Becoming Swedish American.*
45. *Fifty Years of Progress with the First Lutheran Church*, 10.
46. Rosenzweig, *Eight Hours for What We Will*, 113.

47. Karlson, "Swedish Population in Worcester," 26.
48. Ibid., 17–18.
49. Ibid., 26.
50. Parkinson, "Surely These Are My People."
51. "History of the First Swedish Baptist Church of Worcester, Massachusetts."
52. Parkinson, "Surely These Are My People," 7.
53. *Fifty Years of Progress with the First Lutheran Church*, 48.
54. Wahlstrom, "History of the Swedish People of Worcester," 85.
55. Lindberg, *50 Years in New England*, 30.
56. *Worcester Telegram*, May 24, 1948, author's collection.
57. Waldenström, *Genom Norra Amerikas Förenta Stater*, 194.
58. "Trinity Evangelical Lutheran Church," 4.
59. *Worcester Telegram*, April 12, 1975.
60. *This I Believe*, radio show narrated by Edward R. Murrow, CBS, August 29, 1952, http://dl.tufts.edu/catalog/tufts:MS025.006.014.00008.00003.

Chapter 5

61. Hardenby, "När Höganäsarna Gick till Jeppsons Shop."
62. Estus and McClymer, *gå till Amerika*, 7.
63. Sundbeck, *Svensk-Amerikanera*, 28–29.
64. Linn, Dr. Henry. *The Report of the Survey of the Plant Facilities of the Public Schools of Worcester, Massachusetts.* Institute of Field Studies, Teachers College. New York: Columbia University, 1949, 3-5.
65. Folke, "Veni, Vidi Worcester."

Chapter 7

66. Meagher, *Inventing Irish America*, 309.
67. John Ericsson Lodge #25, *Kortfattad Historik.*
68. Diary of Bror Joseph Victor Rosenlund, June 23, 1917, author's collection.
69. Eastern Grand Lodge IOGT, *Historical Review of Activities and Decisions*, 75.
70. Kivisto, "Attenuated Ethnicity of Contemporary Finnish-Americans," 70.
71. Diaries of Bror Joseph Victor Rosenlund, March 1, 1947, author's collection.
72. Letter from Alice Carlson to Bengt Magnusson, July 5, 1983, author's collection.
73. Letter from District Secretary Einar I. Holm to John Ericsson Lodge No. 25 secretary B.L. Hedquist, January 13, 1953, author's collection.

74. Vasa Order of America, *Femtio Års Historik*, 20.
75. Swedish National Federation, *Constitution and By-Laws*.
76. *Petition om svenska språkets införande som valfritt ämne vid hogskolorna i Worcester nu inlämnad*, 1936, author's collection.
77. *Svea*, March 23, 1921.
78. See *Fairlawn Hospital*.
79. Letter from Swedish National Federation to Superintendent Stanley Peterson, October 1, 1965. Records of the Swedish National Federation, author's collection.
80. Tymeson, *As Far West as the Sunset*, 21–22.
81. Millie (last name unknown) in a letter to John (last name unknown), August 31, 1976, Special Collections, Swedish Cemetery Corporation.

Conclusion

82. April R. Schultz, *Ethnicity on Parade*, 89.
83. Kolesar, "Worcester Swedes Entered," 37.
84. Tymeson, *As Far West as the Sunset*, 22.
85. *Worcester Business Journal*, December 20, 1999–January 2, 2000, 82.
86. Zeller, "Changes in the Ethnic Composition and Character," 191.
87. *Auburn Daily News*, February 13, 2012, http://auburn.dailyvoice.com. The Gift Chalet website can be found at https://www.giftchaletauburn.com.
88. Martin and Lorenz, *Our Beloved Sweden*, vi.

BIBLIOGRAPHY

Andreen, Gustav. *Det Svenska Språket i Amerika*. Stockholm: Albert Bonniers Förlag, 1900.

Barton, H. Arnold. *A Folk Divided: Homeland Swedes and Swedish Americans, 1840–1940*. Carbondale: Southern Illinois University Press, 1994.

———. *Letters from the Promised Land*. 4th ed. Minneapolis: University of Minnesota Press, 2000.

Belisle, Alexandre. *Livre-D'or des Franco-Américains de Worcester, Massachusetts*. Worcester, MA: La Compagnie de Publication Belisle, 1920.

Blanck, Dag. *Becoming Swedish American: The Construction of an Ethnic Identity in the Augustana Synod, 1860–1917*. Uppsala, Sweden: Uppsala University, 1997.

Conzen, Kathleen Neils. "Immigrants, Immigrant Neighborhoods, and Ethnic Identity: Historical Issues." *Journal of American History* (December 1979).

Eastern Grand Lodge IOGT. *A Historical Review of Activities and Decisions Made by the Eastern Grand Lodge of the International Order of Good Templars and Affiliated Subordinate Lodges and Auxiliary Organizations*. N.p.: privately published, 1946.

Estus, Charles, and John McClymer. *gå till Amerika*. Worcester, MA: Worcester Historical Museum, 1994.

Fairlawn Hospital: Twentieth Anniversary Expansion Program, 1921–1941. Worcester, MA, 1941.

Femtio Års Historik: Vasa Orden av Amerika. Worcester, MA: Svea Press, 1946.

Fifty Years of Progress with the First Lutheran Church of Worcester, Massachusetts. Worcester, MA: Svea Press, 1931.

Folke, Ellis I. "Veni, Vidi Worcester." *American Swedish Monthly* 52, no. 10 (October 1958).

Gagnon, Richard L. *A Parish Grows Around the Common: Notre-Dame-des-Canadiens 1869–1995*. Worcester, MA: Domus Mariae Inc., 1995.

Gerstle, Gary. "Liberty, Coercion, and the Making of Americans." *Journal of American History* 84, no. 2 (September 1997): 527.

Hanson, Thure. *Swedish-American Souvenir*. Worcester, MA: privately published, 1910.

Hardenby, Brita. "När Höganäsarna Gick till Jeppsons Shop." *Kullabygd* 69 (1996).

Harvey, Anne-Charlotte. "The First Swede in Worcester." *Swedish-American Historical Quarterly* 46, no. 1 (January 1995).

"History of the First Swedish Baptist Church of Worcester, Massachusetts, 1880–1930." Available at Special Collections, Belmont Street Baptist Church.

Johansson, Sven, ed. *Historical Review of Vasa Order of America, 1896–1971*. United States, 1974.

John Ericsson Lodge #25. *Vasa Orden av Amerika, Kortfattad Historik Över en Tjugofem-Årig Verksamhet*. Worcester, MA: Franklin Printing Company, 1925.

Kivisto, Peter. "The Attenuated Ethnicity of Contemporary Finnish-Americans." In *The Ethnic Enigma*. Edited by Peter Kivisto. London: Balch Institute Press, 1989.

Kolesar, Robert J. "The Worcester Swedes Entered." *Swedish-American Historical Quarterly* 46, no. 1 (January 1995).

Lindberg, Luther E., ed. *50 Years in New England: A History of the New England Conference 1912–1962*. N.p.: New England Conference of the Augustana Lutheran Church, 1962.

Linn, Dr. Henry. *The Report of the Survey of the Plant Facilities of the Public Schools of Worcester, Massachusetts*. Institute of Field Studies, Teachers College. New York: Columbia University, 1949.

Ljungmark, Lars. *Swedish Exodus*. Carbondale: Southern Illinois University Press, 1996. Originally published in Sweden under the title *Den Stora Utvandringen*.

Martin, Janet Lentes, and Ilene Letnes Lorenz. *Our Beloved Sweden: Food, Faith, and Flowers*. Hastings, MN: Sentel Publishing, 1996.

Meagher, Timothy J. *Inventing Irish America*. Notre Dame, IN: University of Notre Dame, 2001.

Moynihan, Kenneth J. "Swedes and Yankees in Worcester Politics: A Protestant Partnership." *Swedish-American Historical Quarterly* 40, no. 1 (January 1995).

Nelson, Helge. *The Swedes and the Swedish Settlements in North America*. Reprint, New York: Arno Press, 1979. Originally published, Lund, Sweden: Carl Bloms Boktryckeri, 1943.

Nutt, Charles. *A History of Worcester and Its People*. New York: Lewis Historical Publishing Company, 1919.

Parkinson, E. Malcolm. "Surely These Are My People." 1980. Photocopy, Special Collections, Salem Covenant Church, Worcester, Massachusetts.

Pierson, Karen M. *A Tale of Two Worcesters*. Herefordshire, England: Logaston Press, 1998.

Proko, Barbara, John Kraska and Janice Baniukiewicz. *The Polish Community of Worcester.* Charleston, SC: Arcadia Press, 2003.

Rice, Franklin P. *The Worcester of Eighteen Hundred and Ninety-Eight*. Worcester, MA: F.S. Blanchard & Company, 1899.

Rosenzweig, Roy. *Eight Hours for What We Will*. Cambridge, England: Cambridge University Press, 1983.

Salomonsson, Eric J., William O. Hultgren and Philip C. Becker. *Swedes of Greater Worcester*. Charleston, SC: Arcadia Publishing, 2002.

Salvatore, Nick. *We All Got History.* New York: Times Books, 1996.

Schultz, April R. *Ethnicity on Parade: Inventing the Norwegian American through Celebration*. Amherst: University of Massachusetts Press, 1994.

Scott, Franklin. *Sweden: The Nation's History.* Carbondale: Southern Illinois University Press, 1988.

Spear, Marilyn W. *Worcester's Three-Deckers*. Worcester, MA: Worcester Bicentennial Commission, 1977.

Steinberg, Stephen. *The Ethnic Myth.* Boston: Beacon Press, 1989.

Sundbeck, Carl. *Svensk-Amerikanera, Deras Materiella och Andliga Sträfvanden.* Rock Island, IL: Augustana Book Concern, 1904.

Swedish National Federation. *Constitution and By-Laws.* Worcester, MA: self-published, 1988.

"Trinity Evangelical Lutheran Church: The 50th Anniversary." N.p., 2000.

Trulson, Anton H., and W. Elmer. *Our Viking Industrialists: Who's Who in Viking Industry and Craftsmanship in Northeastern United States.* Worcester, MA: Svea Publishing Company, 1946.

Tulloch, Donald. *Worcester: City of Prosperity*. Worcester, MA: Commonwealth Press, 1914.

Tymeson, Mildred McClary. *As Far West as the Sunset.* Worcester, MA: Swedish Cemetery Corporation, 1961.

———. "The Hinge that Opened the Gate." *Swedish American Pioneer Quarterly* 4, no. 2 (April 1953).

Vasa Order of America. *Femtio Års Historik: Vasa Orden av Amerika.* Worcester, MA: Svea Press, 1946.

Waldenström, Paul P. *Genom Norra Amerikas Förenta Stater.* Stockholm, Sweden: Central-Tryckeriet, 1890.

Waters, Mary C. *Ethnic Options: Choosing Identities in America.* Berkeley: University of California Press, 1990.

Westman, Eric G., and E. Gustav Johnson, eds. *The Swedish Element in the United States*. 4 vols. Chicago: Swedish-American Biographical Society, 1931.

Worcester Board of Trade. *A Tribute to the Columbian Year*. Worcester, MA: F.S. Blanchard and Company, 1893.

Zetterman, Carl, and Frans Lätt. *Kalender Öfver Svenskarne i Worcester*. Worcester, MA: Utgifvarnes Förlag, 1883.

Journals, Newspapers and Publications

American Quarterly.
The Evening Gazette.
A Historical Sketch of Auburn.
Journal of American History.
Svea.
Swedish-American Handbook.
Swedish-American Historical Quarterly.
Worcester Business Journal.
Worcester Evening Post.
Worcester Telegram.

Theses and Dissertations

Balk, Helen Hoppe. "The Expansion of Worcester and Its Effect on the Surrounding Towns." Master's thesis, Clark University, 1944.

Creveling, Harold Franklin. "The Patterns of Cultural Groups in Worcester." Master's thesis, Clark University, 1951.

Karlson, Karl. "The Swedish Population of Worcester: A Study in Social Survey." Master's thesis, Clark University, 1910.

Wahlstrom, Esther. "A History of the Swedish People of Worcester, Massachusetts." Master's thesis, Clark University, 1947.

Zeller, Rose. "Changes in the Ethnic Composition and Character of Worcester's Population." PhD diss., Clark University, 1940.

Local Collections

Belmont Street Baptist Church.
Bethel Lutheran Church.
Bethlehem Covenant Church.
Chaffins Congregational Church.
Clark University.
Emanuel Lutheran Church.
Salem Covenant Church.
Swedish Cemetery Corporation.
Swedish National Federation.
Trinity Lutheran Church.
Worcester Historical Museum.
Worcester Swedish Charitable Association.

INDEX

ABOUT THE AUTHOR

Mr. Salomonsson was born and raised in Worcester, Massachusetts, and became interested in his Swedish roots at an early age. He was a member and spokesperson for the Swedish-American community until his move to Florida in 2005. He served in a leadership role in the following Worcester organizations: the Swedish National Federation, Nordic Lodge No. 611 of the Vasa Order and the Swedish Cemetery Corporation.

In addition, Mr. Salomonsson has co-authored two books on the local community through Arcadia Publishing—*Swedes of Greater Worcester* and *Swedes of Greater Worcester Revisited*—and has written articles that have appeared in Swedish-American publications. He remains dedicated to the preservation of the Swedish Worcester experience and maintains a private collection of material. He is currently a social science teacher at the North Broward Preparatory School in Coconut Creek, Florida.